INITIATE

Powerful Conversations That Lead to Jesus

R. Lee Rogers

Interior Illustrations by Holly Cohick (loagey@gmail.com)

Cover Art by Nicholas Palomo

Edited by Kathleen Dondzila

ISBN: 1500355844
ISBN-13: 978-1500355845

DEDICATION

For every student sharing their faith on the school campus,
and for every youth leader coaching them along the way.

CONTENTS

ACKNOWLEDGMENTS

I must thank my wife for her infinite grace and patience. She was the first to teach me the importance of conversation in a relationship.

I want to thank my conversation partners, who helped me narrow down and select the five conversation models in this book. They are current and former Youth Alive Missionaries and Leaders Richard Baker, Jeff Duvall, Jason Forsman, Rodney Goodlett, Kent Hulbert, Brad Keller, Josh Pearman, Steve Pulis, Forrest Rowell, Ben Russell; Youth Pastors in year one of the Exponential Leadership Cohort Rob Gillen, Bernie Gillott, Steve Hinkeldey, Shane Hotchkin, Andrew Jordan, Kris Lewis, Josh Tarnowski; and one of the wisest and most passionate youth ministry veterans I know—Doug Sayers.

Finally, I want to say thanks to Dr. Joseph Umidi, whose leadership in the Coaching discipline helped me become a better conversationalist and molded many of the concepts found in these pages and in my life.

PART ONE
GETTING READY

ONE
CONVERSATION IS THE KEY

A few years ago a student walked into my office and we had a conversation. He wanted to know about God, or some part of Scripture, or talk about a problem he was struggling with. He didn't grow up in church, and he didn't have a foundation of Scripture or Christianity in his life. I knew God was working on his heart, but I also knew he was far away from God. When he was in seventh grade, someone invited him to a church youth group. He came, and like a lot of students who come to church youth groups, he got involved and even responded to God at the altar. But youth group events, services, and even times at the altar in prayer were not enough to win him fully to the Lord. Like so many people, his life had been complicated from a very young age. He was the son of divorced parents, and his dad was heavily involved in drug and alcohol use. For most of his adolescence he also struggled with drugs and alcohol. He was following in his dad's footsteps; he had little support for his desire for God at home, and all the while a spiritual battle was raging for his soul. Every step he made towards God was met with "flaming darts of the evil one,"[1] designed to destroy the positive growth that was happening in his life.

His name was Eldon, and our conversations became a regular occurrence during those years. At times we had several conversations a week, each one delving deep into life's purpose, God's existence, his struggles, and the meaning of Scripture. There were times during our conversations that I had a very real sense of the war that was raging in the heavens for his soul—I could feel the tension of the battle in the air and in my spirit. The Apostle Paul talks about this secret battle, "For we do not wrestle against flesh and blood, but against the rulers, against the authorities, against the cosmic powers over this present darkness, against the spiritual forces of evil in the heavenly places."[2] Make no mistake, while most of us don't feel it, a war is waging for the souls of mankind, and our friends are no different (we are not exempt, either).

When it came to Eldon, a primary weapon in the war for his soul was conversation. He was very typical of the current generation of young people. He came from a non-traditional family, spending time during the week at both his mother and father's house, and each parent presented different versions of right and wrong. In addition to that, other voices (media, friends, and even the school system) were busy telling Eldon what truth was. Eldon was mostly left on his own to navigate these competing and differing versions of truth, and a church service was just another voice adding to the fray. This is normal for the average young person today; the church is viewed as just another institution declaring its version of the truth. That's one reason why many of them will not visit a church building, attend a service, or listen to a preacher (unless it's at a wedding or a funeral). As Harry Lee Poe stated, "They are not interested in institutions but in relationships."[3] And you can't have relationships without having conversations.

> A war is waging for the souls of mankind.

Over time, Eldon committed himself fully to Christ, and

ended up becoming one of the best evangelists I've ever known. In just a few years of following Jesus, I can personally count over 30 people who made commitments to follow Jesus, or came to church, as a result of his efforts to introduce people to God. Even Eldon's mother and stepdad have started attending church regularly and are connecting to Christ. There were times when I wasn't in the mood to have a conversation with him. Oftentimes, I wondered how long he would continue to struggle with his faith in Jesus, and there were many times when my patience was thin and my frustration was thick. It would have been so much easier if he could've just listened to the sermons, responded, and lived out what was being preached. It would have been so much simpler if, after the first time he showed interest in God or made a commitment at an altar, he didn't continue to struggle with sin and with his faith. I grew up in church, so for me, it was normal to hear a sermon and make a commitment and stick with it. But the truth is, most people need *more* than a sermon or event to make a lasting commitment to Jesus. That is the *new normal* that evangelistically-minded Christians must come to terms with: it's normal for people to need *more* than what church services or events offer—they need relationships built on powerful conversations. Conversation was a key for winning Eldon to Jesus. Years later I would hear him say, over and over again, "The conversations we had were huge in my life. They really made a difference." It's not just Eldon; conversation is the key to connecting most of this generation of young people with Jesus.

Don't get me wrong, I believe in the church and I believe in good preaching. Going to church, listening to a good sermon, or ever preaching a sermon are some of my favorite things to do. But when it comes to leading people to Jesus we must realize the position of the church today is much weaker than it was a few decades

> Conversation is the key to connecting this generation to Jesus.

ago. The church is much less influential than it once was, and most people are less likely to come to church as a result. Not only that, many are also less likely to come to evangelistic church events *unless* they are invited by someone with whom they *already* have a significant relationship. While some people come to Christ in a church service or event, most people will need a Christian to start a conversation with them if they'll ever hear about Jesus.

It's Up To You

It's become popular in the last few decades to be very passive when it comes to faith. In other words, it's trendy to keep your belief in Jesus to yourself. Instead of sharing your faith, an increasingly popular viewpoint is that you should be a good person, love your neighbor, and wait for them to ask about your faith rather than share it openly. We should expect the non-Christian world to push us to be silent about our belief in Jesus, but it's shocking to see this same viewpoint becoming popular in the church. Many proponents of this idea will wrongly use a saying attributed to Saint Francis of Assisi, "Preach the Gospel at all times; when necessary use words." Saint Francis of Assisi never said that.[4] In fact, he was well known for his preaching, his passionate proclamation of Jesus as Lord! To make matters worse, the idea that we should avoid telling people about Jesus, hoping instead that they see our good deeds and come to Jesus in that way, is unbiblical! The Apostle Paul makes it clear in Romans 10 that we must speak with our mouths in order to adequately share the Gospel, "For everyone who calls on the name of the LORD will be saved. But how can they call on him to save them unless they believe in him? And how can they believe in him if they have never heard about him? And how can they hear about him unless someone

> Most people need a Christian to start a conversation with them if they'll ever hear about Jesus.

tells them?"[5] How will any of our friends ever hear about Jesus unless *we* tell them?

That is not to say that your deeds and actions are unimportant, because they are vitally important! I'll talk about that a little more in Chapter 2, but the point here is that we must engage our friends in conversations that lead to Jesus! Michael Green identified three reasons to share the Gospel: [1] God sets the example for us by being the Supreme evangelist (John 3:16) and by empowering his people to become witnesses (Acts 1:8), [2] God has entrusted the Gospel message to us (2 Corinthians 5:19-20), and [3] people who are apart from God are in real need (Ephesians 2:12, Romans 10:3).[6] Bill Bright gave five reasons why "we cannot remain silent":[7]

> We must engage our friends in conversations about Jesus!

- Christ has given a clear command to every Christian.
- Men and Women are lost without Jesus Christ.
- Rather than being 'not interested,' the people of the world are truly hungry for the Gospel.
- We Christians have in our possession the greatest gift available to mankind—the greatest news ever announced.
- The love of Jesus Christ for us, and our love for Him, compels us to share Him with others.

The bottom line is this—it's not up to someone else to start having conversations about Jesus and sharing the faith. It's up to you!

In spite of all that you may see or hear about sharing your faith (or *not* sharing your faith), the truth is people are spiritually hungry. While many don't talk about it, deep inside most people, and especially young people, wonder about spiritual matters and personal relationships. Bill McRaney Jr. lists several questions that young people are asking today about your friendship and their spirituality:[8]

- Do you care about me?
- What is my purpose in life?
- Is there ultimate meaning?
- How can I experience God?
- How can I become God or get right with God?
- Is Jesus the only way to God?
- Do Christian claims match my experience?
- Are gospel essentials real? Do they make a difference?
- Integrity—Does it work?
- Which god is The God?
- What can God do for me?
- Which religion is right for me?
- Which holy book is right?

Think about this: your friends are asking questions just like this deep inside, but they are probably embarrassed to talk about them out loud, or they don't feel like they know anyone well enough to have these kinds of conversations. What if God could use you to have a conversation around these questions that so many people are waiting to discuss? What if God could use you to start a conversation with a friend that ended at the Cross?

> It's not up to someone else. It's up to you.

A few months ago I met a student named Teresa. Teresa was an avowed atheist. She didn't believe in God, and like many New Atheists, she thought religion was evil. She also had a group of friends at her high school who loved God and were committed to sharing their faith with friends like her. This group of friends began inviting Teresa to hang out with them on Friday nights. They started having conversations, and developing great relationships. Along the way they discussed atheism, and the Christians shared their point of view on God's existence. The conversations continued. It wasn't long before Teresa started coming to church. Soon she prayed with her friends and committed her life to Jesus. Today Teresa believes in God and is fully committed to the Cross. She was wondering about these deep spiritual issues all along, and masked her curiosity in atheism. When a group of Christian students took the time to have meaningful and powerful conversations with her, everything changed!

A Different Method for a Different Time

We must have powerful conversations that lead to Jesus if we are to live out the Great Commission (Matthew 28:19) in this generation. Times have changed, and our methods for sharing the Gospel must change with them. Earlier, I shared how the current generation is much less likely to come to church than previous generations were. While we still see some church events in the United States that draw large crowds and a large number of commitments to Christ, very few people today make a *lasting* commitment to Jesus as a result of preaching or evangelistic events. There was a time when that was commonplace; and evangelistic events and altar calls still have a place today, but most people who make a lasting commitment to Jesus at an event like that are only there because someone had already had a conversation with them about Jesus, and the event simply propelled them to the point of decision.

Make no mistake, most people surrender their lives at the foot of the Cross because of "the loving persistence and friendship of someone close to them: a spouse, a friend, a family member."[9] According to the Institute for American Church Growth, 75-90% of new Christians make a commitment to Jesus through a friend who explains the Gospel on an individual, conversational basis.[10] In contrast, only 17% of Christians make a lasting commitment to Christ through an event such as a church service or evangelistic crusade. Even Billy Graham, whose legacy in ministry is the mass evangelism crusade, has stated that mass evangelism is not as effective as when two people have a conversation and one shares about

Jesus.[11] You can invite people to church all day long, wear a Christian T-shirt that proclaims "Jesus is Lord," have the biggest evangelism crusade, or blast Christian music when your friends are in the car, and still see little progress for the Gospel. That's because you're sending out a message, but you're not really communicating.[12] If you want to start making powerful strides for the Gospel, start having conversations. Conversations are the basis for friendship, and most people come to Jesus through a friend.

Getting to Know You

Two-way communication is the key to effectively communicating the Gospel. One reason conversation is vital is because it helps us figure out where people are coming from. It's easy for us to make the mistake that people are like us and see things from the same point of view as we do. When we assume the people we encounter believe what we believe, we've assumed too much. There was a time when someone who wanted to share their faith could make certain assumptions in the United States. For example, here were some commonly held beliefs in the 1950s:[13]

- The Bible was a trustworthy book that could speak to life's problems.
- The church and its leadership were trusted and respected.
- Jesus Christ was largely understood to be the Son of God.
- If someone was "spiritually searching", they were likely searching for the Christian God and the search would involve going to church.

Today our world is very different from the 1950s. Very few of these beliefs are accepted by many in our nation. That same set of statements above look like this today:

- God's existence is called into question. At a minimum, many believe that if God exists, it's unlikely that any single religion is picturing him correctly.
- The Bible is a historical document and contains some wisdom, but can't answer all my problems.
- The church and its leadership are not respected, and are often the subject of suspicion.
- Jesus was a good person who loved people. But he probably wasn't the Son of God, and the miracles he performed probably didn't happen.
- I can search for God wherever I want to. No one can tell me what Truth is, because I can determine it on my own.

Of course, if you're reading this book, you probably don't agree with the above statements. You're likely even offended by some of those statements. You would probably say the following:

- God exists. He created everything.
- The Bible is God's word and can speak to all of life's problems.
- The church is the Body of Christ and is to be respected and embraced.
- Jesus is God's son, died for all of humanity, and everyone can come to God through Him.
- There is only one way to God, and it is through Jesus.

It's good to be sure in your beliefs. But it's a mistake to think that people we want to share our faith with have the same perspective. A conversation can help you discover your friend's perspective, and give you insight on where to start with the Gospel.

Through conversation you can ask questions and figure out what people believe. If you want someone to believe that Jesus is the Son of God, they probably first have to believe that God exists. Believing in God's existence is the foundation of

> It's a mistake to think that people we want to share our faith with have the same perspective as us.

faith, because no one can come to God unless they first believe He is real. If you assume your friend believes in God, you've already made an error. You've got to get to know someone before you can discover where they stand in their belief in God. Getting to know someone by developing a relationship, is the key to effectively sharing the Gospel. And conversation is the key to getting to know someone.

Connecting

Conversation connects us to people in a way that very few things can. A good conversation demonstrates that you care. It's an emotional investment where both you and your friend exchange feelings and emotions, not just information. Dick Innes wrote, "When I give you only words and tell you what I am thinking I am giving only my ideas and thoughts to you. But when I tell you what I am feeling I am giving *myself* to you. This is the heart of effective communication."[14] If you communicate Bible facts, you are communicating Truth. But you're not communicating the whole Truth. The manner in which Jesus affected you is also in play. Has Jesus brought you joy? Changed your life? Delivered your family from drama and pain? All of that can be communicated in a personal conversation.

A good conversation can also help you connect the difference between *felt needs* and *real needs* in your friend's life.[15] As Christians, we recognize that everyone has a very *real need* for Jesus. Hell is real, and avoiding Hell is a *real need* that everyone has. Because we recognize the deep and urgent need to talk about these problems, we almost always want to deal with those issues first. But just because we recognize this very *real need*, it doesn't mean our friends will. If they don't read the Bible, believe in God, or go to church, it's unlikely that Hell is something they think about. They don't see this as a *real need.* On the other hand, there are probably a few needs in their lives that they are really feeling and thinking about. They are likely problems that pale in comparison to the need for Jesus, but nonetheless they are the needs that are weighing most on our friends' minds. Those are called *felt needs.*

> Most people won't be open to talking about their real needs unless someone is willing to listen to their felt needs first.

Felt needs drive so much of what people do in life. The *felt need* for a cell phone, a car, or the latest technology drive people to earn more money to pay for those things. The *felt need* for love, attention, and affection drive many people into relationships before they are ready. The *felt need* for education sends millions of people to college every year. *Felt needs* control much of what happens in life. You know what your friend's *real need* is, but do you know what their *felt need* is? Having a conversation can help you discover their needs, both *real* and *felt,* and understanding their needs can help you share the Gospel more effectively. Most people won't be open to talking about their *real needs* unless someone is willing to listen to their *felt needs* first. Having a conversation can help you connect those needs to the Gospel.

Just Another Evening Stroll

It was just after dinner on a fall evening when Jack and two of his friends took a stroll around their neighborhood, as they did regularly each night. Jack's friends were Christians, but Jack had resisted following Jesus. Still they conversed regularly about all kinds of things in life, occasionally including God and His existence. On that September evening the topic turned to Jesus Christ, and Jack's friends listened intently to his opinions and shared their own; the discussion went on until 3am. A few days later, Jack confessed to having turned his life over to

Christ, largely as a result of that long conversation. He didn't come to Jesus as a result of an event, or because of a church service with inspired preaching, he came to Jesus because two of his friends took the time to have powerful conversations with him.

It was just another evening stroll, yet as a result of those conversations, one of the most powerful and thoughtful writers of the last century became a Christian. Jack was his nickname; his real name was Clive Staples Lewis. C.S. Lewis went on to write many popular Christian books, including the children's series *The Chronicles of Narnia* and many classics like *Mere Christianity*, *The Screwtape Letters*, and *The Great Divorce*. The committed Christian friends who held those long conversations with him were Hugo Dyson, a fellow professor, and J.R.R. Tolkien, who went on to write *The Hobbit* and *The Lord of the Rings*. The writings of C.S. Lewis have had a profound impact on the world, leading many to the Cross of Christ, and strengthening the faith of many Christians. I can't help but wonder—what would have happened if Dyson and Tolkien hadn't taken the time to have those conversations with Jack, or were too intimidated or polite to talk about Jesus, or decided to let their deeds speak for the Gospel instead of using their voices to communicate the Truth? The conversations were the difference maker. It can be the same for you and your friends. What if someone like C.S. Lewis is waiting for you to have a conversation with him about Jesus?

This book is designed to help you have powerful conversations that can lead to Jesus. It's divided into two parts: "Preparing for Conversations" and "Five Powerful Conversations." Read through the first part thoroughly before you start the second. Earning the right to be heard, the role of faith, the Holy Spirit, and the components of great conversations are all foundations to understand and practice before trying out the five conversations in Part Two. The goal of this book is to help you become a great conversationalist who can develop strong relationships that connect to the

Gospel, not to memorize new evangelism techniques. Every conversation you have will be a little bit different, but if you learn the basics, you can navigate all kinds of discussions and still end up at the Cross.

---

[1] Ephesians 6:16b ESV
[2] Ephesians 6:12 ESV
[3] Harry Lee Poe, *Christian Witness in a Postmodern World* (Nashville: Abingdon Press, 2001), 34.
[4] Mark Galli, "Speak the Gospel. Use Deeds When Necessary," ChristianityToday.com, http://www.christianitytoday.com/ct/2009/mayweb-only/120-42.0.html?paging=off (accessed June 24, 2014).
[5] Romans 10:13-14 New Living Translation, Second Edition
[6] Michael Green, *One to One: How to Share Your Faith With a Friend* (Nashville: Moorings, 1995), 7-8.
[7] Bill Bright, *Witnessing Without Fear: How to Share Your Faith With Confidence* (San Bernardino, CA: Here's Life Publishers, 1987), 38-48.
[8] McRaney Jr., *The Art of Personal Evangelism: Sharing Jesus in a Changing Culture* (Nashville: Broadman & Holman Publishers, 2003), 128.
[9] Green, *One to One*, 11.
[10] William Fay, *Share Jesus Without Fear* (Nashville: Broadman & Holman Publishers, 1999), 12.
[11] Green, *One to One*, 12.
[12] Dick Innes, I Hate Witnessing: A Handbook for Effective Christian Communication (Upland, CA: Acts Communications, 1995).
[13] McRaney, 123.
[14] Innes, I Hate Witnessing, 154.
[15] Ibid, 155.

TWO

EARNING THE RIGHT TO BE HEARD

A few years ago my pastor got a vision to start a police chaplaincy in the local police department of my town. It didn't take long to get off the ground; a few pastors in the community signed up to become chaplains and I was one of them. We rode "shotgun" with local police officers, usually on the 3-11 shift, and served police, victims, and even perpetrators by providing a spiritual presence at moments of trauma and emotion. It was a great way to serve the town and individuals impacted by negative circumstances in life. It was also a front row seat to the drastic consequences sin can have on families, communities, and even emergency responders. One Friday night I decided to ride along on the "tactical shift." This was a special shift that took place from 7pm-3am each night. It was specifically designed to target some of the darker crimes, such as drugs and prostitution, which were taking place in the small town my church was located in. Friday night after 9pm in a police car can be a pretty wild ride!

I was the first chaplain in the program to ride along on this shift; most chaplains went home by 11pm. Sometime after we chased drunk drivers, served arrest warrants, and shut down a bar brawl, the officer I was riding with turned to me and excitedly said, "You're like...YOU'RE THE LATEST CHAPLAIN EVER!" He was enthralled that I took enough of an interest to ride along with him into the darkest hours of the night. No chaplain had done it before. It wasn't long after that when he showed up at our church for the first time. I hadn't pressed him to come to church, and I hadn't even gotten to the point where I was comfortable sharing the Gospel with him yet. But I did meet some of his needs, some of the needs of the community, and in the process I had made an impression. I earned the right to be heard before I started sharing what was truly on my heart—the Gospel.

A few years after the police chaplaincy got rolling our pastor's vision expanded, and he started a few new chaplain programs in our town; emergency medical services chaplains, hospital chaplains, nursing home chaplains, and even bar chaplains! Instead of just pastors being chaplains, the people who attend our church now receive the necessary training to be chaplains themselves. The goal is always the same—be a spiritual presence in crucial areas of the community where pain is experienced. Today, on any given Sunday, you will find our church filled with emergency medical technicians, police officers, nurses, and people who first came into contact with our church in bars, handcuffs, and on ambulance stretchers. None of them first came into contact with our church through hearing a sermon, reading a tract, or attending an outreach. Instead, the people in our church served the needs of the community and its people, and in their service they earned the right to be heard.

Now let me tell you a different story. About 10 years ago my wife and I bought a house and moved in. We started to meet the people in our neighborhood, and as a devout Christ-follower, I prayed that I would be able to introduce my neighbors to Jesus. We weren't in the house more than a few months when the roof started to leak, and because we didn't have a lot of money, I decided to fix it myself with the help of some friends. Not only was I short on money, I was also short on time. I only had one weekend relatively free, and even then I had a very small window of opportunity to work on the roof. We started working on a Friday night around 9pm and worked until 11pm. Then we were back up on the roof early Saturday morning at 6:00am. I needed to get that roof fixed, and I was going to do what it took to make it happen!

Now if you know anything about roofing, you know that it's quite loud. To make matters worse we live in a fairly narrow valley, so every loud noise echoes off the mountainsides for miles around. All kinds of scraping, prying, banging, and creaking goes on when you're replacing a roof! We started tearing the old roof off on Friday night, and even though it was loud, I didn't think my neighbors minded. It was Friday night, after all, and people do tend to stay up later. On Saturday morning we began work at 6am. I needed to have the entire old roof cleared off by 7am, when some additional help was arriving to help me put on the new roof. So early on that September morning, the neighborhood was filled with sounds of old shingles being ripped off, nails being pried out, and lots of debris being thrown off the roof. Bang! Crash! Creak! And on and on it went for about 30 minutes.

Around 6:30am I heard a voice I somehow didn't expect to hear. It was an angry voice! I looked down from the roof and there stood one of my neighbors holding a cup of coffee and dressed in a bathrobe. She wasn't there to compliment us on a good job; on the contrary, she gave me a strong piece of her mind. Not only had we woken her early on a Saturday morning, but we had also kept her up late on Friday night. She'd had all she could take, and now she was letting me know how irritated she was. I was mortified. As a follower of Christ it's my strong desire to live at peace with my neighbors and to give them every opportunity to see Jesus living in me. But as a homeowner pressed for time, I had allowed my need for a new roof drive me to become an irritation to my neighbors. Instead of showing my neighbors how Christ changed my life, I showed them how annoying a neighbor I can be! And in the process, I constructed a barrier to a good relationship with my neighbor. I also constructed a barrier to the Gospel.

Instead of earning the right to be heard, I had earned the right to be shunned and yelled at! It took me several years to gain back a good relationship with that neighbor (more on that later). More importantly, it took me several years to get the relationship back to the place where I could openly share the Gospel without being an irritant. I cannot stress this to you enough—the way you live your life, treat your neighbors, serve your community, and love those you come into contact with will either earn you the right to be heard, or build a barrier towards people receiving the Gospel. You may be reading this book because you're ready to share your faith and excited to talk to your friends about God, but if you aren't living and serving like Jesus commanded, you aren't representing Him well. If you want to start having conversations about Jesus, you'd better make sure you've earned the right to be heard.

> The way you live your life will either earn you the right to be heard, or build a barrier towards people receiving the Gospel.

Loving Out Loud

Did you know that God loves everyone? Did you know that it is not His desire that anyone should perish, but that everyone would come to know Jesus and place their faith in Him (2 Peter 3:9)? That means every neighbor, classmate, and person we meet is another soul that Jesus died for. God loves everyone, and we are to follow His example (Ephesians 5:1). That means we cannot love God and be obedient to Him without loving the people God places in our lives. If we are sincerely giving ourselves completely to God, we will love all the people God loves.[1]

Have you ever thought about what Jesus came to earth to do? Knowing what Jesus came to earth for, and how He accomplished it, teaches us how we can become more like Him. A lot of people think Jesus came to make people moral. In a sense this is true, because Jesus death on the Cross erased our sin before God, and so we were made holy through His sacrifice. But He didn't come to make us moral people, He came to sacrifice, and our holiness was a result of that sacrifice. We observe morality that comes as a result of knowing Jesus, but becoming like Christ is not about being morally upright and ethically straight; morally upright and ethically pure people are to be found in many religions and walks of life. Learning to be like Christ means learning to live a life of sacrifice because that is what Jesus came to the earth to do, and moral uprightness and ethical purity come as a result of sacrificial living.

Living a life of sacrifice means that we must love out loud. Loving out loud means that we must learn to serve others. Loving out loud means we love with a purpose—to draw people to God and to the church. We love people, not because we get something out of it, but because God loves people. Jesus came to the earth with an agenda—to seek and to save that which is lost (Luke 14:2). Everything He did moved Him closer to that goal, which was accomplished on the Cross. He loved out loud, and caused a stir while doing it, and in loving out loud He demonstrated the true nature of God. We must serve our communities and try to bring healing just as Jesus did. We must learn to consider others before we consider ourselves. If we are not representing Christ in this way, then we have not earned the right to speak His message, for we are not truly representing who Jesus is.

Living on Purpose

The manner in which we live often communicates our message before we even open our mouths. When I was up on that roof at 6:00am, I was clearly communicating that I didn't care if my neighbors were woken up early. I communicated selfishness and a lack of love for my neighbors. What a horrifying witness! But when I was riding around as a police chaplain, volunteering to help the community, I was communicating that the church cares about people, and that I was there to serve. If our message is about God's love, then we must live on purpose so this love is demonstrated. Our style must match our message!

Oscar Thompson wrote about the failure of some preachers to make their style match their message:

> "Some are able evangelists in the pulpit who inspire many people to make decisions for the Lord. Yet, I have watched these same men act rudely toward a waitress or a salesperson and be first-class, carnal Christians. A Christian has no excuse for this. What does the world see in your daily life? Do they see Jesus?"[2]

Has anything like that ever happened to you? One Sunday morning I had the chance to accompany a pastor and his family to lunch after church. It was one of the pastor's favorite restaurants and he ate there often. The staff knew who he was and we were in our "Sunday best," so the waitress certainly knew we were church people. Something didn't go quite right with the order, and soon a member of the pastor's family

> The manner in which we live often communicates our message before we even open our mouths.

started behaving very rudely to the waitress. I was so embarrassed, because it was such a poor example of the true kindness that is found in Jesus. Why would anyone want to come to church if the church is full of rude people like that? Why would anyone want to associate with Jesus if His followers treat people badly over simple mistakes? This is why it is so important that we live out loud—earning the right to be heard starts with our daily interactions with every person we encounter!

The Apostle Paul knew this truth well. He wrote to the young church planter, Titus, and instructed the church on the island of Crete, "to be obedient, to be ready for every good work, to speak evil of no one, to avoid quarreling, to be gentle, and to show perfect courtesy toward all people" (Titus 3:1–2 ESV). It's easy to segment your life so that you are rude to people without knowing it. For example—do you make eye contact with the cashier at the gas station? How about your waiter or waitress? How about the lunch lady? Are you rude to your teachers, or have you realized that God also loves them, and that you should show them God's love just as much as your friends? What do your daily interactions say about your relationship with God?

Jesus was an amazing man—He was a powerful teacher, healer, and He paid the price for our sins on Calvary. But He was also a carpenter. He worked with wood and He made things and sold them or traded them with the people in His town. How do you think Jesus treated His costumers? Did He cheat them? Of course not! Did He do less than His best work for them? Of course not! Did He look them in the eye and smile? He probably expressed God's love better than any other human in history. Ninety years after His death and resurrection, one of the early church fathers named Justin Martyr wrote about Jesus' reputation as a carpenter.[3] Justin wrote about the plows and yokes that Jesus made, and how He used them as examples in His teaching. Jesus healed people, taught crowds numbering in the thousands, spoke to Kings and governors, died on a cross and was resurrected—and somehow people still remembered His carpentry and the things He made. He must have been pretty good at it! If Jesus took the time to do even everyday work tasks like carpentry well, shouldn't we also pay attention to the details of our lives?

Painting a Picture

The details of our lives—how we treat people and go about our business—is as important as the words we say! When we treat people well, we earn the right to be heard. When we treat people rudely, we earn the right to be ignored. In *Out of the Saltshaker & Into the World*, Rebecca Pippert wrote, "The way we treat others reveals what we think God is like...People will understand as much of the love of God as they see in our own lives. The first Bible many people will read will be your life."[4] If it's true that our lives portray God's love—what do people think about God after observing your life? We all paint a picture with our actions, and this is a visible generation that loves pictures! In 2013, Instagram grew in active users by 23%. In the same time period, Facebook declined by 3%.[5] Why is that? Because we love to look at pictures! So what kind of picture are you painting with your life?

About 100 years after Jesus left the earth His followers were growing at a rate that alarmed government officials. The government considered Christianity to be an offshoot of the Jewish religion, and didn't consider Judaism or Christianity to be a good fit for the Roman Empire. Emperor Hadrian was ruling at that time, and he was no friend to the Jews. He built a temple for himself on top of the ruins of the first-century Jewish Temple in Jerusalem. The Jews revolted against Hadrian and Hadrian went to war against them. In the backdrop of all

You are painting a picture with your life.

this fighting was the emerging Christian religion, which was closely tied to Judaism. One of the leaders of Christianity was a Greek living in Athens named Aristides. He wrote a letter to Emperor Hadrian to convince him not to persecute the Christians. First, he painted a picture of what Christians were like by describing their morality. He said they didn't lie, commit adultery, or have sex outside of marriage. They were honest with money, honored their families, judged righteously and treated others like they wanted to be treated. He essentially said Christians were good moral people.

But Aristides really made his case when he painted a picture of Christians as deeply compassionate and loving citizens. He wrote:

> "He, who has, gives to him who has not, without boasting. And when they see a stranger, they take him in to their homes and rejoice over him as a very brother...And whenever one of their poor passes from the world, each one of them according to his ability gives heed to him and carefully sees to his burial. And if they hear that one of their number is imprisoned or afflicted on account of the name of their Messiah, all of them anxiously minister to his necessity, and if it is

> possible to redeem him they set him free. And if there is among them any that is poor and needy, and if they have no spare food, they fast two or three days in order to supply to the needy their lack of food."[6]

> What kind of picture are you painting with your life?

Doesn't that paint a picture of the kind of people you'd want to be like? Their love and compassion had earned them the right to be heard, and the results are hard to argue with. In the first three centuries of Christianity the church had grown from a small band of disciples to over 6,000,000 people![7] Would someone describe your love and compassion for others in the same way Aristides described the early church? What kind of picture are you painting with your life?

Becoming Useful—A Practical Truth

One way of earning the right to be heard is to become useful to our friends and neighbors. Not only should we become useful, but we must also demonstrate how the Gospel is useful in everyday life. We live in a time when people embrace and believe in whatever is working for them, and if Christians and the church are a drain to them, or a useless part of society, then it's unlikely they will want anything to do with Jesus. In other words—Christianity needs to be practical! Will McRaney Jr. wrote, "Notwithstanding the influence of the Holy Spirit, people will give their lives to Christ as it fits into their perspective and values."[8] We have to show that Christianity "fits" in order for it to be accepted, and that means we need to show that serving Jesus is useful.

Jesus was a master at being useful to those around Him. Often, when he approached a town or city, large crowds would come out to meet Him. They were hoping for healing or life-changing wisdom—and they frequently got what they wanted.

There's nothing more useful to the sick than healing, so it's no wonder Jesus' popularity grew. Mark 2:1-12 tells the story of men who brought a paralytic to see Jesus. They were so desperate to get their friend healed they lowered him through the roof. This story teaches us a lot of things: Jesus' power to heal, his popularity, and the desperate need of so many of the people who hadn't yet been in contact with Christ. But the biggest lesson for us is how useful Jesus had become—useful enough that people were willing to break through the roof in order to see Him. You can also learn this—when you begin to meet the needs of your community with power and effect, people will do almost anything to find out what's driving you.

It's tough to argue against something that works, and if Christianity "works" then people will be more likely to agree with it. Simply put, if the Gospel isn't helpful or useful, it cannot find traction. On the other hand, if Christianity is shown to be useful or helpful to someone's life, then at least some of it has to be accepted as being true. I call this "practical truth." When the Gospel is practically true, it's not simply true because of what I say or think; it's true because of what people are experiencing. When the Gospel becomes practically true, full belief and commitment to Christ isn't far away!

The key to demonstrating Christianity as "practical truth" is not changing the message, that would be terribly wrong, but changing the method of how the message is communicated. The Apostle Paul did this all the time, and wrote about it in 1 Corinthians 9:19-23 (HCSB):

> Although I am a free man and not anyone's slave, I have made myself a slave to everyone, in order to win more people. To the Jews I became like a Jew, to win Jews; to those under the law, like one under the law—though I myself am not under the law—to win those under the law. To those who are without that law, like one without the law—not being without God's law but within Christ's law—to win those without the law. To the weak I became weak, in order to win the weak. I have become

> all things to all people, so that I may by every possible means save some. Now I do all this because of the gospel, so I may become a partner in its benefits.

Paul was willing to change his methods as he went to different kinds of people so that he could share a message that never changes—that Jesus was God's Son and came to connect men to God. Rather than just proclaim that Jesus was God's Son, Paul was willing to show the practical truth of the Gospel, and in doing so he won many people to the Truth of the Gospel.

When Paul was proclaiming the message among Jews, "he was kosher," and when with Gentiles, "he was nonkosher," for "neither mattered to God."[9] This is great news for us today, because people accept things into their lives based upon how useful they are, and we are free to make the Gospel useful to them. Paul showed genuine humility through his choice to change his methods for each group he wanted to reach. He truly made himself a slave to everyone. He even becomes "weak" for those who are weak. He was not afraid of making the gospel practically truthful to those who believed and behaved in ways that were different from him. This humility towards a greater cause is something the Church lost when Christianity became popular, but is certainly something we could stand to regain today. Start by asking the question, "Am I useful to the people I want to reach?" If you're not useful, you haven't earned the right to be heard.

> Am I useful to the people I want to reach?

A Cup of Water—In the Name of Jesus

A few years ago I traveled to Tanzania as part of an effort to drill clean water wells in remote tribal villages. We traveled to a Masai village called Lobersoit. Masai communities are suspicious of outsiders, and typically not welcoming of those beyond the tribal community. However, the Masai also have a problem the church has begun to bring healing to—a lack of good clean drinking water. It's estimated 43% of Sub-Saharan African children drink unsafe water, and 1 out of 5 will die before the age 5 as a result.[10] Several years ago, a man started an organization called WorldServe that raises millions of dollars each year and funnels the money into MajiTech, a company that drills wells all over Tanzania and Kenya for the benefit of the Gospel. They offer a cup of clean water in the name of Jesus.

While the Masai are usually suspicious of outsiders, when we arrived at the village of Lobersoit, we were greeted by hundreds of Masai warriors in parade formation, some having traveled hours to greet our group with celebration. Why? Because Christians drilled a sustainable deep and fresh water well to serve a tribal community and bring healing. Their attitude towards outsiders (Christians) and towards non-tribal religion (Christianity) has been radically changed by the practical truth of the Gospel. Not only has the attitude changed, but the story being told about Christianity has also changed. Practical truth teaches that those who drilled the well brought healing and life—and they were Christians motivated by the Gospel! The village has also welcomed a school and medical clinic, also provided by the same Christian witness. A church has started and is thriving under the leadership of a Masai warrior who became a pastor.

While in Tanzania I also spoke with a missionary who had served in that field for over 30 years. He shared that in the southern regions of Tanzania, Islam dominates the landscape and has never been pierced. For over 30 years, missionaries have tried to plant churches in areas like Dar es Salaam, but every effort has failed and nothing has come of it. Christians have been forcibly thrown out of Muslim villages. Recently, however, the situation has taken a dramatic turn. Christians have begun to drill wells in Muslim villages, and the ruling imams have agreed to allow churches to be planted and Christianity to be proclaimed. The practical truth of fresh water, a healing source that is saving the lives of Islamic children in southern Tanzania, has demonstrated the truth of the Gospel. The story of Christianity among the Muslims there is changing.

Changing the Story

Have you ever been drawn in by a powerful story? What about someone's opinion? Has someone's opinion ever swayed you when making a decision? Whenever I want to buy something off the Internet, I always try to read the reviews of the product I'm buying. Almost every product has some kind of review online, and most will have several comments from different buyers. A review is simply someone's experience with the product—his or her story of how well the product worked (or didn't work). If a product worked well, it gets good reviews and I'll probably buy it. But if the product didn't work well, there will be a lot of negative reviews, and I know to stay away from it. The overall story of each product is determined by the story of those who bought and experienced it. This is how truth works today—it's determined by the story of each person and their experiences. We know Christianity is true, but others will need to be convinced by their own story, by their own experiences.

In any given culture, truth is whatever the group "story" of that culture says it is. James Sire said it like this, "Truth is whatever we can get our colleagues (and our community) to agree to."[11] If truth is determined by the collective story of each community, then it's time we start determining what that story will be through the practical truth of the Gospel. The healing power of the Gospel, and a church that goes out of its way to serve and sacrifice for others, must become the biggest story in every community. C.S. Lewis wrote, "I believe in Christianity as I believe that the Sun has risen, not only because I see it, but because by it I see everything else."[12] Practical truth is like the Sun at daybreak. Before the form of the sun even peaks over the horizon, its light begins to expose the world around us and shows us things that weren't previously visible.

What if all your neighbors knew you were the person who could be called upon to help in a time of trouble? That's practical truth. What if all the students in your school knew that you were the kind of person who would buy lunch for someone when they forgot their lunch money? That's practical truth. What if every school could count on the faith community to help it meet budget shortfalls? That's practical truth. What if the church provided a father for every fatherless child, and a mother for every child in need of a mother's love? What if Christians were the first to respond to international disasters? What if the church committed to ending world hunger and providing clean water and education for every child in the world? And what if, alongside all of this, Christians were passionately and faithfully proclaiming the love of God and the reconciliation of man to God through Jesus Christ? How would the landscape of every school and community change if Christians arrived with a demonstration of the Spirit and of power through practical truth? What would happen if every believer earned the right to be heard?

---

[1] Scott T. Jones, The Evangelistic Love of God & Neighbor: A Theology of Witness & Discipleship (Nashville: Abingdon Press, 2003), 51.
[2] W. Oscar Thompson Jr., *Concentric Circles of Concern: Seven Stages for Making Disciples* (Nashville: Broadman & Holman Publishers, 1999), 15.
[3] Justin Martyer, *Dialogue of Justin, Philosopher and Martyer, with Trypho, a Jew*, Chapter 88, in *The Apostolic Fathers With Justin Martyr and Irenaeus*. vol. I of *The Ante-Nicene Fathers*. Edited by Alexander Roberts, et al., Accordance electronic ed. (New York: Christian Literature Company, 1885).

[4] Rebecca Manley Pippert, *Out of the Saltshaker & Into the World* (Downers Grove: InterVarsity Press, 1979), 76.
[5] Kate Knibbs, "Instagram Grows Faster than Facebook, Survey Says," *Digital Trends*, http://www.digitaltrends.com/social-media/instagram-is-growing-faster-than-twitter-facebook-and-pinterest-combined-in-2013/, (accessed April 1, 2014).
[6] Aristides, "The Apology of Aristides the Philosopher" in Vol. X of *The Ante-Nicene Fathers*, Ed. Allan Menzies (Grand Rapids: Wm. B. Eerdmans Publishing Company, 1951), 276-278.
[7] Rodney Stark, *The Rise of Christianity: A Sociologist Reconsiders History* (Princeton: Princeton University Press, 1996), 6.
[8] Will McRaney Jr., *The Art of Personal Evangelism* (Nashville: Broadman & Holman Publishers, 2003),
[9]Gordon D. Fee, *The First Epistle to the Corinthians*, from *New International Commentary on the New Testament*, ed. by Ned B. Stonehouse (Grand Rapids: Eerdmans, 1987), 427, Accordance electronic ed.
[10] UNICEF, "UNICEF - Water, Sanitation and Hygiene - World Water Day 205: 4,000 Children Die each Day from a Lack of Safe Water," UNICEF, http://www.unicef.org/wash/index_25637.html (accessed December 3, 2013).
[11] James Sire, *The Universe Next Door: A Basic Worldview Catalog*, Kindle electronic ed. (Downers Grove: InterVarsity Press, 1997), location 2489.
[12] C.S. Lewis, *The Weight of Glory* (Harper Collins e-books, 2009), 140, Kindle electronic ed.

THREE
FACTORING IN FAITH

One of my favorite movies when I was a teenager was *Indiana Jones and the Last Crusade*. This movie had everything a good movie has—adventure, action, mystery, history, a treasure hunt, a love story, and comedy. In this third installment of the Indiana Jones movie series, Indiana is teamed up with his father (Dr. Henry Jones) to find the Holy Grail. The Holy Grail is the legendary cup Jesus Christ drank out of at the Last Supper with the disciples, and it was used by Joseph of Arimathea to catch Christ's blood on the cross. It's highly unlikely that any of that is true—but it really makes for a great story! The legend of the Grail, in this particular movie, holds that whoever drinks from the cup will be given eternal life on earth—they will never die. As if the story wasn't interesting enough already, Indiana and Henry are in a race against the Nazis to find the Holy Grail. If the Nazis find the grail, they will rule over the earth in evil forever, but if Indiana finds it, the Grail will find a proper home as a historical artifact in a museum. More importantly, the world will be saved from the evil Nazis.

One of the more interesting parts of the story is the difference between Indiana and his father, Henry. They share the same goal—finding the Holy Grail—but they approach the quest from far different perspectives. Indiana is a college professor and archeologist who believes in cold-hard facts. He repeatedly claims, in all of the movies, that he doesn't believe in legends, "hocus-pocus," magic, or superstitions. In the beginning of the movie, Indiana stands up in front of his college class and states, "Archeology is the search for fact...not truth. If it's truth you're looking for, Dr. Tyree's philosophy class is right down the hall." Indiana Jones claims to be a man of fact, a man of science. His father, on the other hand, readily accepts things on faith. While a bit of a bumbling and clumsy man, he comes off as more experienced and wiser than his scientist son. The Holy Grail has been a lifelong search for Henry, and he describes the quest as giving him "illumination." Refuting his son's approach to finding the Grail, Henry says, "The quest for the grail is not archeology, it's a race against evil. If it is captured by the Nazis the armies of darkness will march all over the face of the earth." Henry, while also an archeologist, is more a man of faith than of fact. And so in *The Last Crusade*, a classic drama between faith and fact unfolds.

One of the climactic points of the movie comes as Indiana and Henry approach the final stage in locating the Holy Grail, a series of three life-threatening puzzles located in a canyon in the desert. Unfortunately, the Nazis had caught up with them and shot Henry in the stomach. Because they were out in the desert, and because the wound was so severe, the only hope for Henry was to receive water from the Holy Grail, so Indiana had to traverse the three life-threatening puzzles on his own. The final of the three puzzles involved a fascinating challenge of faith that forced Indiana to step out of his comfort zone of facts and wander into the realm of unseen realities. After facing death in the first two challenges, Indiana walked through a dark stone hallway to emerge in an opening of a sheer cliff. He couldn't turn to the left or right. Directly across from him, approximately 50 feet, was another sheer cliff with an opening. There was nothing but an empty chasm between the two openings; a chasm so deep the bottom was not visible, so wide no man could jump it. There was no way to get across.

This final challenge was called "The Path of God," and the clues that led Indiana to this point indicated that a "leap of faith" would be required to get across. Knowing that it was impossible to jump the distance, but faced with his father's death if he didn't get across, Indiana placed his hand on his heart, raised one foot into the air as if to take a giant step, and allowed his body to fall forward! But instead of falling deep into the chasm to his death, Indiana's raised foot came down on something solid, yet invisible. His leap of faith had paid off! He slowly made his way across to the other side, where he turned and threw a handful of pebbles behind him onto the invisible path. The pebbles scattered across the invisible walkway, revealing a stone bridge that had been constructed to blend in with walls of the chasm. It was there the whole time, yet it couldn't be seen by the human eye.

This is what faith can be like! Faith is like taking a giant leap into something you don't see; yet you possess the belief that it is there. I don't see God, but I believe that He exists. I didn't see Jesus die on the cross, but I believe that He did and that what happened there made a way for me to be right with God. Hebrews 11:1 states, "Faith is being sure of what we hope for and certain of what we do not see." We often treat our salvation, the Bible, and our relationship with God as facts. We believe them to be undeniably true. But the reality is these are facts we accept on a basis of faith—and that's okay. For example, God and I did not sit down at a table and sign a contract agreeing to my salvation through the sacrifice of Jesus Christ. I have never met God face-to-face, and I didn't actually see Jesus , either. However, I believe the Bible is true, that it represents God's contract with all of humanity, and that Jesus did die as a sacrifice that was accepted by God on my behalf. But I have no proof other than my belief. Ultimately, if our friends are going to accept Jesus as Lord, they will have to possess the same kind of faith. As Hebrews 11:6 says, "Without faith it is impossible to please God, because anyone who comes to Him must believe that He exists and that He rewards those who earnestly seek Him."

It's important to understand two crucial facets of faith when it comes to sharing Jesus with our friends. The first thing to understand is that all of us come to Christ as a matter of faith, not based on fact. When we go through school we are trained to think in terms of facts and scientific observation, but this has little to do with coming to Jesus. After all, "It is by grace you have been saved, through faith—and this not from yourselves, it is the gift of God" (Ephesians 2:8). The second thing to understand about faith is that it can take a long time to gain it. This is especially true for people who trust in facts, what they see with their own eyes, and scientific observation. It can be extremely difficult for a "concrete thinker" to believe in something they do not see. But that does not mean it's impossible for this kind of person to possess faith, it only means that it may take them a while to arrive at that conclusion.

Faith and Fact

We learn things in a very linear fashion. Let me explain that; we learn that almost everything in life happens in order. Our lives flow like a timeline of events that progress in order.

For example, no one grows old before they've been young. Everyone is a toddler before they become a teenager. Life happens as a line of events, one after another. History is the same way. We know that Columbus is credited as the first explorer to discover the American continents, and that most of Europe was not aware of the "New World" until his voyages. Therefore, no lasting European settlements existed in America *before* Columbus' fated journey of 1492. It wasn't until *after* 1492 that large amounts of Europeans started coming to the American continents. It was a sequence of events that flowed in order. History is an ordered line of events where one thing leads to another.

We learn things in a very linear fashion.

In math class we learn the logic of the universe. Math teaches us that things should always add up. Science teaches us the facts behind how the universe works. Everything has an explanation, and everything has an order. Sometimes we begin to think this way about our faith. We start believing that we can explain everything, that everything in our faith has a scientific explanation, and that Scripture and God's existence can be proven like any scientific fact. The only problem with this kind of linear and scientific thinking is this—even in the scientific world, everything *doesn't* always add up, and there isn't *always* an explanation for everything. Real life teaches us differently.

For example, have you heard of the Big Bang theory? A Roman Catholic priest, who was also a scientist, named Georges Lemaître was the first to propose this theory, better known as the theory of the Expansion of the Universe. Through observation and measurement, scientists had begun to understand that the universe is expanding outward from a central starting point. If the universe is expanding outward from a central starting point, that must mean that all of the universe at one point in time had exploded out from that central location with such force that it still moves outward today. And that is the Big Bang theory: the matter of the universe expanded suddenly outward from a hot and extremely dense state. Although the Big Bang theory offers an explanation of how the universe came into its current state, there are many questions it leaves unanswered. For example, where did the hot dense matter come from? What caused it to be so hot? What forced it to be so dense? Where did the energy come from that infinitely expands the universe? Could it really have just existed? Or was it created? The truth is, science can't explain *everything*, and everything doesn't *always* add up. A lot of Christians are afraid of the Big Bang theory, but they shouldn't be. The Big Bang theory serves as a great scientific explanation of Genesis 1—a factual, scientific, yet partial understanding of how God created the universe.

The truth about our faith is this: we can't explain *everything* in terms of facts and science. That's okay! That's what faith is! Faith, while reasonable, may not be scientifically rational. Think about the book of Exodus, when Moses was leading the Israelites out of Egypt. Pharaoh and the Egyptian army were in hot pursuit, and Moses and the Israelites had run into a dead-end at the Red Sea. They were up against the water and the Egyptians were closing in fast. Scientifically, rationally, and linearly, this should have spelled doom for the Israelites. But faith changes the outlook! Irrationally, nature behaved in a way that was logically impossible and the Red Sea parted. This miracle makes no scientific sense, although science has tried to make sense of it. We are taught to reason through logic, observation, and linear thinking. But Scripture, and our own experience, teach us that things do not necessarily need to make sense in order for us to believe in them. Everything *doesn't* always add up, and there isn't *always* an explanation for everything. That's where faith comes into play.

> Science can't explain *everything*, and everything doesn't *always* add up.

This is so crucial for us to understand as we try to have conversations with people about Jesus. We do not need to prove God's existence (we will talk about that later in this book) in order for someone to believe in Him. After all, *you* believe in God even though you've never seen Him. If we could prove God, then faith wouldn't be necessary at all. You don't need faith to believe in something you see—your eyes tell you it exists and logic wins the day. But when you don't see something, like God, yet you believe God exists, faith ultimately wins the day. Stop trying to prove everything you believe! We don't come to Jesus on the basis of *fact*. We come to Jesus as a matter of *faith*. It's okay if we cannot prove every part of our faith to those we have conversations with.

It probably won't be long after you start having conversations about Jesus that someone will try to stump you with an unanswerable question. Don't let that bother you. In fact, unanswerable questions are helpful to us as we try to persuade our friends to accept a life rooted in faith. It's okay to not know all the answers. In fact, that can be used to engage people in further conversations. *They* don't know the answers either. So don't get defensive if you don't know an answer. Be thankful that the question has been asked, because it will give you an opportunity to research things. Rebecca Pippert writes, "I often tell people I'm very grateful that God is using them to sharpen me intellectually when I am stumped by a question. I tell them I don't know the answer but can't wait to investigate it. And usually I do investigate and learn in the process."[1] And if it truly is an unanswerable question, that only proves the need for faith.

> Stop trying to prove everything you believe. We don't come to Jesus on the basis of *fact*. We come to Jesus as a matter of *faith*.

> If it truly is an unanswerable question, that only proves the need for faith.

One final note on the idea of faith and fact; don't be afraid of facts, even if they seem to disprove your faith. If the fact is true, then God already knows it and it fits into His creation perfectly, even if it seems to contradict our current understanding. Two early Christian thinkers, Justin Martyr and Augustine, came to the realization that all truth is God's truth. In other words, if something is scientifically and factually true, then it has to fit somehow with God's created order. God can't lie, and all truth belongs to Him. So if a scientific fact is presented that seems to contradict your faith, there are only two possible ways to think about it. First, it is possible that the scientific fact is actually flawed or is misunderstood in relation to the laws (both discovered and undiscovered) of nature. Remember, everything *doesn't* always add up, and there isn't *always* an explanation for everything. Second, it's quite possible that *we* do not quite understand how God has worked in nature, or that we understand Scripture in a way that's different from the way God has intended. In other words, we must have faith that if something is really true it fits into God's plan, even when we don't understand how.

Faith Grows Over Time

The second element of faith that is important to understand when it comes to conversations about Jesus is this: faith takes time to grow. We often think of salvation as a one-time experience that happens instantly, as if it's a decision that occurs in an instant. But frequently, accepting Jesus as Lord is a process that takes place over time as someone grows in his or her ability to have faith. Jim Petersen describes evangelism in farming terms. He states, "I…expanded my understanding of evangelism to include planting, watering, and cultivating as well as reaping. I learned that evangelism is a process."[2]

I love that farming analogy! My grandfather was a farmer.

Pap grew the best sweet corn I've ever tasted. Ever since I was a little kid I loved going to his farm. Sometimes I got to ride on the tractor, and sometimes I got ride on the planter behind the tractor as the seeds were planted in the ground; and later I got to ride on the wagon when the crops were harvested. When I grew up and was married and in college, we didn't have a lot of money, and when I went to visit Pap he would load me up with lots of homegrown vegetables to take home. My Pap knew how to make things grow! Right into the last year of his life, he would plant, water, cultivate, and reap. Every day he would be active in checking the plantings, or bringing in the harvest, or sorting out the weeds. I got to see and understand the lengthy process it takes to grow delicious vegetables.

When the harvest came in, Pap would sell his crops from his wagon on the side of the road. He would lounge in a chair against a tree and wait for customers to stop by. One of my favorite memories is sitting out there with him, helping him bag vegetables, and talking to customers as they stopped by. He was always grateful for the business, and would sincerely say, "Thanks for stopping!" as the customers drove off. I wonder how many of those customers appreciated the amount of work that had gone into the food they walked away with. Very few people grow their own food anymore. Most of us go to the grocery store when we need vegetables. We get what we need instantly. We don't have to plant it, water it, cultivate it, or harvest it. We simply buy it. But what Pap did wasn't as simple as going to the grocery store. What Pap did took time. Sometimes we want our friends to come to Jesus instantly—like going to the store to buy food. But more often than not, faith takes time to grow and develop—like a farmer who grows delicious vegetables.

Have you ever seen an annoying ad on television that runs over and over and over again? I'm talking about the kind of advertisement that asks you to call in to a 1-800-number to purchase the product at the end of the commercial. ShamWow, Pocket Hose, Flex Seal, Perfect Bacon Bowl, and the list could go on and on. Believe it or not, there's a method to the madness of repetition. Marketing experts believe that you must hear about a product around seven times before you will actually purchase it.[3] So they play the same ads over and over and over again. And it works! I am not suggesting that you make the Gospel into an annoying advertisement that plays over and over, but I do want you to understand that people must come into contact with something repeatedly before they will believe it. And the Gospel is no different. The average person must hear the Gospel 7.6 times before they develop faith to believe in Jesus.[4]

When you pour your heart out to a friend, but they don't come to a point of faith in Jesus, that doesn't mean your efforts were fruitless. That may only be the first, second, or even fifth time they've had contact with the Gospel. Faith takes time to develop. Remember, the Gospel is not just about making a decision to go to heaven and not to go to Hell. It's far more life altering than that. When someone comes to Jesus, it should change their entire life, view of the world, actions, and relationships. Most people need to think about it before they're ready to come to faith.

Sometimes we feel the intense pressure to "close the deal" by having someone accept Jesus and pray a prayer of faith in our first encounter. What if we never see them again? What if something happens to them before they have another chance to hear about Jesus? By all means, do all you can to share the Gospel, but don't get so aggressive as to scare them off. Remember, you are not the only person God is using to impact the world. God will place other believers and circumstances in their path. In Corinth, the Apostle Paul and a guy named Apollos both played a role in bringing the Corinthians to Jesus. Paul wrote, "I planted the seed, Apollos watered it, but God has been making it grow. So neither the one who plants

> Faith takes time to grow and develop.

nor the one who waters is anything, but only God, who makes things grow. The one who plants and the one who waters have one purpose, and they will each be rewarded according to their own labor. For we are co-workers in God's service; you are God's field, God's building" (1 Corinthians 3:6-9 NIV).

I'll never forget a girl from my high school. She was bright and cheery, a talented athlete, and an all-around fun person to be with. She wasn't a Christian, but she knew that I was. I would carry my Bible around my high school, try to talk to my friends about Jesus, and generally tried to be an upright example of what it meant to serve Christ. I wasn't a perfect example, but I was trying my best to be a good Christian. She was a year or two ahead of me in school, and she graduated without coming to know Jesus. Several years later, I had graduated college and started youth pastoring. I was attending a statewide youth ministry event with thousands of other people. I was hanging out with my youth group in a skating rink at a late-night event, when I ran into this same girl from my high school. I was shocked to see her there! She wasn't a Christian in high school, but she must have become one if she was attending a church youth ministry event like this.

After the initial shock, surprise, and happy greetings I couldn't help but ask the question that was pounding in my head. "So...what are you doing here?" What I was really asking was, "You're a Christian?! How did that happen?" She began to tell me her story. A few years prior she had started attending a local church near Philadelphia with her boyfriend. It wasn't long after that when they came to faith in Jesus, and soon following they got involved as youth leaders in their church youth group. I was thrilled! But it was what happened next that really got my attention. She said, "I've been doing a lot of thinking about the people God placed in my life who planted seeds along

> "Thank you for everything you did in high school to share the Gospel."

the way that helped me become a Christian later. You were definitely one of them. Thank you for everything you did in high school to share the Gospel." I couldn't believe it. Faith takes time to develop, and one plants, one waters, but God makes it grow.

When it comes to sharing the Gospel, having conversations about Jesus, and attempting to lead our friends to the cross, we must always keep in mind how important faith is to the process, and that faith is the very nature of our relationship with God. But that kind of faith can take time to develop, and we must always remember that accepting Jesus is a process that may happen quickly, or may take days, weeks, or even years to happen.

One plants, one waters, but God makes it grow.

---

[1] Pippert, 128.
[2] Jim Petersen, *Living Proof: Sharing the Gospel Naturally* (Colorado Springs: NavPress, 1989), 62.
[3] McRaney, 166.
[4] Fay, 11.

FOUR
THE HOLY SPIRIT

The other day I had two very interesting conversations with two fascinating, but very different people. The first person I conversed with was the air conditioning repairman. I cut the refrigerant line on my air conditioner a few weeks ago and all the cold stuff leaked out, so he had to spend several hours at my house making the repair. Since he was going to be there a long time, I thought I would strike up a conversation. We had never met before, so I wasn't sure how it would go, but I thought I'd take a shot at getting to know him better and look for a way to connect him to Jesus. We ended up talking the entire time he was there—nearly three hours! We started with small talk, and as I listened to the details of his story, I was able to ask him more and more questions about his life. His name was Chris and he lived in the next county, just over the mountain range.

Chris looked a little rough around the edges. He had a dragon necklace, a few piercings, a chin-beard that extended 4-5 inches and was somewhat forked in appearance, and he had a tattoo sleeve running up his right arm. The tattoo was pretty intimidating. There were images of skulls, snakes, and demons. I couldn't see the whole picture because the sleeves of his uniform covered up about half of the tattoo. Still, it was evident that he and I ran in pretty different crowds. I didn't let that stop me from engaging him in conversation. It didn't take long for me to feel comfortable asking him some personal questions, and it didn't take long for him to begin telling me his life story.

Chris and I went to competing high schools around the same time, so our conversation started there, with small talk, but soon it got pretty personal. He has been married for over 10 years and is raising three teenagers, with another child in college. He is not their biological father; they are his wife's kids from another marriage. However, it was evident that he cares deeply for them and has been their father for most of their lives. He was wearing four motivational bracelets and I asked him about each one. They were all bracelets made to support his friends and family who are battling cancer. The story he told me about himself painted a picture of a caring and compassionate individual, but it was not what I was expecting from the tattooed and pierced man who stood in my yard fixing my air-conditioner, and I told him so.

"You know Chris, you look pretty tough on the exterior, but I think inside you're just a big softie. You've been a loving father to the fatherless, and you are compassionately supporting your friends who have cancer." Chris replied, "Well...believe me I used to have a pretty hard edge." Then he started to give me some of the darker details of his life. It turns out Chris's dad died when he was around one, and his stepdad used to beat him regularly. As a teenager, Chris started to hit the weight room and joined the football team. He excelled on the field, and was soon awarded a scholarship to play football in college. Then one rainy day he lost control of his car, crashed in an embankment, and his spine was crushed. For the next 18 months he had to go to therapy to learn to walk again, needed help going to the bathroom, and couldn't bathe himself. He lost his football scholarship, and with it his dreams of a college degree.

Back on his feet and mad at the world, Chris turned to drugs, alcohol, and fighting to cope with his difficult circumstances. Burning bridges with his family, getting kicked out of bars for fighting, and with very little hope, it wasn't long before Chris hit rock bottom. I couldn't believe the nice guy I'd been conversing with about family and football was the same guy who had been abused, paralyzed, and was a recovering alcoholic. I was intrigued because he had obviously overcome all these challenges and was in a pretty healthy place today. I asked him what woke him up at rock bottom, and what had caused him to have such an astounding recovery from all these tragedies. I was expecting to hear a story about God, faith, or the church. But instead, he said his grandmother had died, and he didn't get a chance to say goodbye because his alcoholism had destroyed their relationship. Broken and lost, he picked himself up and began to set his life in order.

I was really surprised that God wasn't a part of his story somewhere. I prodded him a little more, asking, "Did religion play any role in overcoming your challenges?" He said, "No," and then explained a little further. He believed that God existed and that God had protected him and had a plan of some kind for his life. But he had also tried going to church, and instead of finding a welcoming environment, the church began to lay out "rules" of how to be a Christian. They told him what he couldn't listen to, what he couldn't do, and tried to make him fit into their lifestyle in order to make him a "proper" Christian. It was just too much for an abused, formerly paralyzed, alcoholic to take. He was looking for God, but instead found rules. He decided to give up church altogether. While trying to convince him of how to be a good Christian, the people in the church instead convinced him the Body of Christ wasn't for him.

The amazing thing about this story is God was clearly working on Chris's heart. He overcame extremely difficult circumstances, became a loving father and friend, harbors no bitterness at God, and readily recognizes God's existence and protection in his life. But the people in the church tried to convince him that his lifestyle was wrong, and in the process they may have short-circuited the work of the Holy Spirit in

Chris's life. Let me be clear—there were certainly many parts of Chris's life that were not in line with Biblical principles for serving Jesus—that is not in question. However, there is a problem with understanding the role of the Holy Spirit in evangelism, the salvation of man, and how God draws people to Himself. There are times when it is appropriate for Christians to approach other believers regarding their conduct and life decisions. Jesus talks about this in Matthew 18:15-17, and Paul talks about this in 1 Corinthians 5, and 2 Thessalonians 3:14-15. But all of those passages deal specifically with "brothers," or people who have already committed their lives to Jesus and who are also committed to the church. When it comes to those who are outside the church, it's God's job, through the Holy Spirit, to convince them to change. As the Apostle Paul wrote at the conclusion of a passage on church discipline, "What business is it of mine to judge those outside the church? Are you not to judge those inside? God will judge those outside" (1 Corinthians 5:12-13a NIV).

Let the Holy Spirit do the Convincing

This is the first big idea I want you to understand when it comes to the Holy Spirit and having conversations about Jesus—it's the Holy Spirit's job to convince people to change, not yours. Jesus laid this out plainly for us in John 16 when He was speaking with the disciples about His departure from the earth and the coming of the Holy Spirit. He said, "When He (the Holy Spirit) comes, He will convict the world of its sin, and of God's righteousness, and of the coming judgment" (John 16:8 NLT). In other words, the Holy Spirit does the hard work. While we may be responsible to bring correction to our brothers and sisters inside the church, it is the job of the Holy Spirit to convince people outside the church (the world) of

> When it comes to those who are outside the church, it's God's job, through the Holy Spirit, to convince them to change.

their sin and God's righteousness. The word "convict" in this passage means to say that someone has done wrong, and that there is proof of wrongdoing.[1] It is a conviction associated with crime, fault, error, or sin and suggests the shame of the person who was convicted.[2] To convict someone means they are *convinced* beyond all doubt that what they were doing was wrong. That's really hard to do!

Has anyone ever tried to convince you that you were wrong about the way you were living your life? Most people aren't open to that kind of discussion. In fact, most nonbelievers will get offended and may no longer talk to you if you tell them their lifestyle is wrong or sinful. That's exactly what happened to Chris. I would be afraid to share Jesus with anyone if I thought it was my job to convince him or her to change. It's just too difficult! I believe that's the reason God made it the Holy Spirit's job; it's just too difficult for man to do. There is really only one person who can convince people of their sin and God's righteousness—the Holy Spirit. When we try to do a job that clearly belongs to the Holy Spirit, people like Chris get turned off to the Gospel. But when we allow the Holy Spirit to do the convincing, God changes lives in ways we could never imagine.

> It's the Holy Spirit's job to convince people to change—not yours.

The same day I had this long conversation with Chris, I had a second conversation with man named Art. I've known Art for a few years; he's around retirement age and he's been a Christian for a few decades. Art had a pretty checkered background before he came to Jesus. He was a rescue diver in the Vietnam War, was a heavy drinker, smoker, and was constantly getting into brawls. We sat around a living room and Art started to tell me a little bit about how he came to know Jesus, how he started going to church, and how his life dramatically changed after all that happened. Up until that moment in his life, Art knew about Jesus, but had decided he

> There is really only one person who can convince people of their sin and God's righteousness—the Holy Spirit.

just wanted to live life on his own terms. In those days, a lot of churches were more conservative than they are now. You couldn't really be a part of a church if you drank any alcohol, smoked cigarettes, or gambled. Those were all things Art wanted to do, so he just figured he wouldn't be a Christian. Art turned to me and said, "Have I ever told you what caused me to stay in church and become a Christian?" Then he started to tell me the story.

Art married a young lady named Joyce, and Joyce started attending a church near their home in California. She wanted Art to go to church too, and even though he didn't want to, he humored his wife and went to church with her once in a while. Art really couldn't stand Christians. He found them to be judgmental and self-righteous, and that was one of the biggest turn-offs to becoming a Christian. Still, he occasionally went to church with Joyce. He didn't mind this church too much because, even though they were very conservative, they didn't tell Art what he should and shouldn't do. One day Art and Joyce went out to eat with the Pastor after the service. Sitting around the table, the Pastor turned to Art and said, "Art, I'd really like you to consider becoming a member of the church."

Art was dumbfounded. He couldn't understand why the Pastor would want him to become a member of the church. He began to think of all the things he was doing in his life that went against the Christian lifestyle. He was pretty sure the Pastor knew about all of it, so he was confused why the pastor asked him to become a member. Art responded, "Pastor, I don't think that's such a good idea." The Pastor said, "Why not, Art? I think you'd be great." Art responded, "Pastor, for starters, the members of your church don't drink, they don't smoke, and they don't gamble. I do all of those things." The Pastor looked

Art in the eye and said, "Art, just join the church, become a member, and the Holy Spirit will take care off all that. " Art was astonished.

He did just what the Pastor suggested, and the Holy Spirit began to work in Art's life. In ways that Christians never could, the Holy Spirit began *convincing* Art to change his life and become a fully devoted follower of Jesus and member of the Body of Christ. Later, Art would become an ordained minister and a pastor, impacting thousands of lives. Today Art and Joyce live in Tijuana, Mexico, where they serve as full-time missionaries. They've started two orphanages, helped the church in Mexico construct dozens of churches, and they've had an immeasurable impact on the community around Tijuana. Art was not convinced to change by an argument, by a Christian who pointed out his sin, or by a pastor who tried to get him to obey a set of rules. The Holy Spirit convinced Art of his sin and God's righteousness. The Holy Spirit convinced him to change.

I am so thankful I am not the one responsible to convict people of their sin, or convince them to change their ways. As Ken Gaub wrote, "Don't tell people what they need to change in order to become a Christian. When a person accepts Christ, he becomes a new creature. God will clean him up; he will change for the better (believe it or not, without your help)."[3] That really makes sharing the Gospel so much easier by removing the pressure to win an argument, or to force people to see what they're doing wrong and make them agree to change. Frankly, none of us are in a position to point out anyone else's wrongdoing, because we ourselves continue to struggle with sin (Romans 7:14-20). As Jesus said, "Let any one of you is without sin be the first to throw a stone..." (John 8:7 NIV). Even if we did have the right to convict people of their sin (which we don't), how could we know everything that needs to change in anyone's life? It's impossible! I thank God for the Holy Spirit, who searches all things (1 Corinthians 2:10), and guides those who believe in Jesus into all truth (John 16:13). So stop pointing out others' sins, and starting pointing to Jesus. Let the Holy Spirit do the hard work.

Although it's not our responsibility to convince people to change, that doesn't mean that we don't have a part to play in leading people to the Cross. We play a huge and important role in making Jesus known throughout the world, and especially to our closest friends. We are called to proclaim the Gospel to all the earth, the whole creation (Mark 16:15)! It's our job to talk to people about Jesus. After all, no one can believe in God unless they've heard about Him, and they won't hear about Him unless someone tells them (Romans 10:14). God has entrusted the message of the Cross to us, and we are Christ's representatives (2 Corinthians 5:19-20). Although we don't convict people concerning sin and righteousness, we do try to persuade others that God is real and that Jesus died for them (2 Corinthians 5:11). We must proclaim the truth of Jesus Christ, and let the Holy Spirit do the convincing.

Stop pointing out other people's sins and start pointing to Jesus. Let the Holy Spirit do the hard work.

The Holy Spirit: The Original Evangelist

There's more good news—the Holy Spirit helps us in proclaiming the Gospel. We are not on our own, left to our own ideas and thoughts when talking to people about God. We don't even have to rely only on our own experiences and knowledge to communicate the Gospel. God is already drawing all of humanity to himself through the Spirit. This is the second big idea I want you to understand when it comes to the Holy Spirit and having conversations about Jesus—the Holy Spirit is already having a conversation with all the people of the earth, trying to convince them to believe in God, but most people don't recognize that the conversation is happening. Jesus said the Holy Spirit, when sent to the earth by the Father, "will testify" about Him (John 15:26). In other words, the Holy Spirit is the original evangelist—declaring Jesus and the Gospel to all the earth in ways we do not understand.

> The Holy Spirit is already having a conversation with all the people of the earth, trying to convince them to believe in God.

That's great news for us! It means most people will be open to a discussion about God because they will likely have some inner understanding of God's existence, their need for a connection to God, and if we listen closely enough we may even pick up on how the Holy Spirit has been speaking to them. For example, remember Chris? He's the air-conditioning repairman from the beginning of this chapter. Chris didn't grow up with any teaching about God, he was beaten and abused, paralyzed, and was a recovering alcoholic, but he still believed God was real and had protected him. Where did he get this understanding? I asked him why he believed God was real. Chris responded, "I don't know. But it's like I can feel Him. I know He's real." The Holy Spirit is testifying to Chris, and Chris doesn't even know it!

That's why Rebecca Pippert states, "We must never assume that a person will not be open to Christianity."[4] The Holy Spirit is continually conducting a case for Christ throughout the whole world, speaking to every person about Jesus.[5] That means even the coldest, meanest, cruelest person you know is being spoken to by the Holy Spirit. That means the Holy Spirit has already spoken to every person you have a conversation with about God. It means you are not alone in trying to have a conversation with an unbeliever about God. The Holy Spirit has already been

> The Holy Spirit has already spoken to every person you have a conversation with about God.

testifying about Jesus, is currently testifying about Jesus, and will continue to testify about Jesus after your conversation has ended.

Power to Be a Friend, Power to Have a Conversation

The third big idea I want you to understand when it comes to the Holy Spirit and having conversations about Jesus is power—the power to be a witness. Jesus told his disciples in Acts 1:8 that they would receive power when the Holy Spirit came on them, and out of that power they would be witnesses for Him. Jesus' words came true in Acts 2 when the Holy Spirit came upon the disciples on the day of Pentecost in Jerusalem. At nine o'clock in the morning, Peter stood up before a crowd of visitors from many regions of the Roman Empire and shared the Gospel. He was full of the power of the Holy Spirit, and the Holy Spirit gave him a compelling message to speak. The church was born that day, and three thousand people came to believe in Christ for the forgiveness of their sins.

The power of the Holy Spirit in the life of a believer is the power to be a witness for Christ. Imagine...the same Spirit that raised Christ from the dead dwells in you and is empowering you to talk to people about Jesus! The disciples knew this power well and through the Holy Spirit the Gospel was spread across the Roman Empire and into many different cultures during their lifetimes.[6] So how do we do this? How do embrace the power of the Holy Spirit to be a witness? It's simple; we take initiative in friendship and in conversation, and then we let the Holy Spirit work through us.

> The power of the Holy Spirit in the life of a believer is the power to be a witness for Christ.

If you want to fulfill the Great Commission, to make disciples of all nations, you first need friendship, because discipleship almost always works through relationship. The Holy Spirit can help you with this. Jim Peterson notes four stages in building a friendship: (1) taking the initiative, (2) establishing rapport or some kind of bond, (3) being a friend, and (4) building a relationship.[7] Friendship always starts with someone taking the initiative in conversation. The Holy Spirit can help you take the initiative, and the Holy Spirit can help you have a great conversation that establishes friendship *and* leads to Jesus. The Holy Spirit empowered the disciples to perform miracles, heal the lame and the sick, and to cast out demons, and so much more (Acts 3:6-8, 5:12, 16). But in a much more subtle way, the Holy Spirit was at work in empowering them to speak to strangers, giving them words to say, and boldness to take initiative. Just as the Holy Spirit worked through the disciples for mighty acts of power, so the Holy Spirit can help you to take the initiative in friendship and in conversation.

Friendship always starts with someone taking the initiative in conversation. The Holy Spirit can help you take the initiative.

So much of how the Holy Spirit interacts with you, as a believer, involves speaking to other people. In 1 Corinthians 12, the Apostle Paul names nine gifts that come from the Holy Spirit. Five of the nine gifts deal directly with speaking: the message of wisdom, the message of knowledge, prophecy, tongues, and interpretation of tongues.[8] The message of wisdom and the message of knowledge happen when the Holy Spirit gives you a piece of information to share with another person; wisdom pertaining to the future, and knowledge pertaining to the past or present. A lot of people believe prophecy means predicting the future, but a prophecy is simply a message from God, spoken by a believer through the power of the Holy Spirit. Have you ever felt like God gave you something to say or to share with someone? That's a prophecy, and it may have been a message of wisdom or knowledge, as well. Now I'm not suggesting that you go up to every person you want to talk to and say, "Thus sayeth the Lord..." and proceed to give them a message from God in a strange voice or in a strange way. That would be weird. But I am telling you this—the Holy Spirit can give you words to say and give you insight on how to have a conversation with someone.

Jesus stated that under certain circumstances, when we're in trouble for the Gospel or when we need to defend ourselves, the Holy Spirit will teach us what we should say (Luke 12:12). The point is this—the Holy Spirit can help you take the initiative in conversation because the Holy Spirit works through your voice and speaks to your mind by giving you words to say, even if you think you've got nothing to say. I didn't think I had anything in common with Chris, the air-conditioning repairman. He played football in high school, while I was in musicals and sang in the chorus. He repairs machinery for a living, and I mostly sit at a desk and work from a computer. He and his wife are raising four kids, and my wife and I only have dogs. He has tattoos and piercings, and I've never had anything like that. I'm not sure how I could've started a conversation with him apart from the influence of the Holy Spirit. In my natural skill and ability, I would probably be too intimidated to even talk to him. But through the power of the Holy Spirit, I was able to take initiative.

> The Holy Spirit works through your voice and speaks to your mind by giving you words to say, even if you think you've got nothing to say.

Within two hours of meeting him for the first time, Chris had shared intimate details about his life; his family and the challenges of being a stepdad, some of the darkest parts of his personal history and how he overcame them, his alcoholism and the tragic loss of a loved one that woke him from his downward spiral. That's not normal! Very few people, if anyone, would share details so intimate with someone they'd just met, let alone a random appliance repair customer. It was a powerful conversation, but only because it was shaped through the power of the Holy Spirit. I also knew the Holy Spirit had been at work in his life, testifying in some way about Jesus, because the Spirit is at work in the same way through all people. Knowing that helped me look for clues to how God was working in his life already, which is how I found out about his belief in God and lack of belief in the church. And at the end of the day I shook hands, not with a repairman, but with a new friend. Prayerfully, that friendship will continue and I will be able to have more conversations that will lead to Jesus.

Summary

In this chapter, I shared three big ideas about the Holy Spirit and having conversations about Jesus. First, it's the Holy Spirit's job to convict people about their sin and God's righteousness. Ultimately, people will only change when they're personally convinced their actions are wrong, and it's the Holy Spirit's place to do the convincing, not ours. We shouldn't make a big deal about people's sin; we should make a big deal about Jesus. The Holy Spirit will take care of the rest. Second, the Holy Spirit is already having a conversation with every person about Jesus, testifying on His behalf and bearing witness to His work on the Cross. We can be sure the Holy

Spirit is already drawing every person we have a conversation with to God, and if we listen we may be able to pick up clues as to how the Spirit is at work. Third, the Holy Spirit gives us power to be a witness by speaking to us and through us. We can take the initiative and have powerful conversations through the power of the Holy Spirit, even if we have nothing in common with the other person. We are not alone when we talk with others about Jesus. The Holy Spirit is our ally, and is working to draw all men to the Cross.

---

[1] Greek-English Lexicon of the New Testament Based on Semantic Domains, "ἐλέγχω ἔλεγξις ἐλεγμός," Accordance electronic ed., 436.

[2] Thayer's Greek-English Lexicon of the New Testament, "ἐλέγχω," Accordance electronic ed.

[3] Ken Gaub, *What's Your Passion? Proven Tips for Witnessing to Anyone* (Green Forest, AR: New Leaf Press, 2004), 57.

[4] Pippert, 115.

[5] Leon Morris, *The Gospel of John*, New International Commentary on the New Testament. Accordance electronic ed. (Grand Rapids: Eerdmans, 1995), 607

[6] Jones, 41.

[7] Petersen, 120.

[8] A great book on 1 Corinthians 12 and the gifts of the Spirit is Harold Horton's *The Gifts of the Spirit* (Springfield, MO: Gospel Publishing House, 1975).

FIVE
GREAT CONVERSATIONS

You'd have been hiding under a rock if you didn't notice the technological shift that's taken place in the last ten years. Not only is our society more mobile, but we're also more connected. All sorts of social networks exist to connect people together: Facebook, Instagram, Twitter, Pinterest, Google+, and the list could go on and on. The amazing thing about all this connectivity is that many people feel less connected than ever. That's because social networks have helped us get connected, but they haven't helped us develop real friendships. Social networks let us see what's happening in each other's lives, but social networks can't initiate a *conversation* about what's happening in each other's lives. Only we can do that. In some ways, all this connectivity and technology has made it even more difficult to talk to one another.

A few years ago I received a set of noise canceling headphones for Christmas. Later that evening my wife and I were sitting in the living room; I was on the couch surfing the Internet on my computer, and she was on the loveseat surfing the Internet on her computer. I had my new headphones plugged in and they worked great! I couldn't hear anything other than what was coming through the headphones. While I was sitting there my wife was trying to talk to me, but I had no idea. She said my name a few times, raising her voice a little bit each time, louder and louder, but I couldn't hear her. I just kept staring at the computer screen. I was surfing Facebook when a message notification popped up. It was from my wife, and it read, "Hello over there!" I looked up, and we both laughed. There we were, sitting just feet from each other, but unable to have a conversation. That's what social networking is like a lot of the time—you can see each other, but there's no meaningful conversation. And where there's no meaningful conversation, there's no meaningful relationship.

That is one of the great challenges of the current generation—we have connectivity, but we do not have meaningful relationships. That's also a unique challenge for the church, because as we read in Chapter One, the majority of people who become Christians do so through a friendship or another meaningful relationship. But it doesn't *have* to be a challenge, because we can make it our advantage instead. In this highly mobile society, where the extended family has crumbled and the

> Where there's no meaningful conversation, there's no meaningful relationship.

traditional nuclear family is diminishing, good relationships are highly valued because they are more and more difficult to come by.[1] So if we can learn how to develop great relationships, we will not only bring value to our friends by giving them something they are looking for, but we will have a much better chance of leading them to Christ through those relationships than through any other means. The need for meaningful relationships is hidden deep inside the DNA of all mankind. God said it best in Genesis 2:18, "It is not good for man to be alone."

So how can we learn to develop great relationships? By having great conversations! A few years ago I heard Dr. Joseph Umidi say, "The currency of the Kingdom of God is relationships. The currency of relationships is conversation."[2] If you can learn to be a great conversationalist, you can have great relationships. If you can have great relationships, you can make a major impact for the Kingdom of God. Learning to have a great conversation is the first step in sharing your faith. Oftentimes, we get that reversed. We're so eager to share our faith, but we don't understand how to have a meaningful conversation with someone. This chapter will focus on some principles for having great conversations. Great conversations are others-centered, involve powerful questions, and they're propelled forward through listening and responding. Best of all, anyone can learn to have a great conversation!

Elements of Great Conversations

Great conversations are others-centered. Will McRaney Jr. writes about three different styles of communication that are used in sharing the Gospel. They are *self-centered, message-centered,* and *others-centered.* [3] *Self-centered* conversation means the focus is on you—the person doing the talking. If you take a self-centered approach to conversation, you'll likely be unaware of the needs and reactions of your conversation partner, and you're likely to communicate with fear and uneasiness. *Message-centered* communicators do not focus on themselves or others, but on the message they want to get across. Message-centered conversations are typically one-sided—meaning only one person does the talking, and that person only talks about one thing; his or her message. That's not really a conversation at all, and it's not a basis for relationship. This conversation style isn't very popular today because most people you'll want to share the Gospel with will consider relationships more valuable than a message—even a message of Truth. The third kind of communication is *others-centered.* In an others-centered conversation, you focus on your conversation partner. An others-centered conversation shows respect, care, and compassion for the person on the receiving end of the conversation.

If you want to have a great conversation, you need to stop talking about yourself and your message, and start focusing on the other person. This may seem like the opposite of what you want to do. After all, this book is about conversations that can lead to Jesus. So why not focus on the message? Why not focus on what God has done in your life? First, remember, you have to earn the right to be heard. When it comes to conversation that means you have to focus on others for a long time before you talk about yourself. Second, when a person can only talk about his or herself, or his or her message, it's really annoying. It's unlikely anyone will want to have more conversations with you if you only talk about yourself or your message.

> Great conversations are others-centered.

A few years ago I was hosting a weekly golf game at a local course early in the morning. There was an open invitation for a lot of the guys I knew to play. I wanted to get to know some of them better, and have some fun on the golf course at the same time. One week a man showed up who hadn't been before. I was looking forward to getting to know him better, but soon I became exhausted with talking to him. The reason he came out to play golf was to try to get me to invest in his business, and that was all he could talk about. He spent the whole time, several hours, trying to sell me on his investment. I asked about his family, his work, his hobbies, but he refused to talk about anything other than this great moneymaking investment he was offering me. It actually wasn't a moneymaking investment, and I knew it, so I wasn't going to buy in. I politely declined his offer several times, but he persisted with his message. Exhausted with talking to him, I finally said, "My friend, I'm just not going to buy in, so can we talk about something else?" He angrily replied, "Don't call me 'friend' if you're not going to listen to my message!" Wow! I was shocked! I couldn't believe our friendship was dependent upon me buying into his message. The golf game ended on a sour note, and our relationship also hit a sour note. It has never fully recovered.

If all you can talk about is yourself and your message, even if it's the Gospel message, you're likely exhausting the people you're talking to. Not only that, but you're communicating that you don't care about them, their dreams and ambitions, or anything in their life. You're communicating that you only want to talk about the things you care about, and you may be communicating that you only care about yourself. That's the opposite of what you want to say! Is that the kind of person *you* want to spend *your* time talking to? Of course not! If you want to become effective in having conversations that lead to Jesus, you need to become the kind of person someone wants to talk to more than once, and that means having others-centered conversations. So how do you have an others-centered conversation? Learn to ask powerful questions.

Great conversations are built on powerful questions. Most conversations are formed largely by the questions that are asked, so if you want to have a great conversation you must start by asking great questions.[4] Great questions don't have an agenda behind them. They aren't asked to get a specific answer, but instead show real interest in the other person. When you ask a question that shows a genuine and informed interest in your friend, or in their opinion, you have paid them a very high compliment.[5] However, when you ask a question that has an agenda behind it, also called a "loaded" question, you're only using your friend to accomplish your agenda. A loaded question is one that is designed to steer the conversation towards your agenda, a specific answer, or that establishes a fact or assumption that someone may not have agreed to.

For example, if you ask a friend, "Are you still wandering aimlessly through life without God?" you've asked a loaded question. Firstly, it's loaded because you are fishing for a specific response that will help you accomplish your agenda. Secondly, you're making the assumption that his life is aimless without God. You may see it that way, but he probably does not, and by asking this loaded question you've probably insulted him. There is a time for that kind of question, but if you're new to the relationship, or if you haven't earned the right to be heard, it's best to stay away from loaded questions. You could find out the same information by asking a question that doesn't assume anything and isn't agenda based by saying, "So, how's life? Tell me what's going on with you." Not only is that an unloaded question, it's also a question that shows genuine interest in another person, instead of just showing interest in your agenda. In the process, you'll likely find out the information you wanted to know anyway. As Michael Green said, "One of the best ways to start a conversation is to ask a question—an unloaded one!"[6]

Jesus was great at asking powerful questions. He knew how to get a conversation going. Tony Stoltzfus compiled the following list of powerful questions that Jesus asked:[7]

- What's this you're discussing so intently as you walk along? Luke 24:17
- What do you seek? John 1:38
- What is written in the law? How do you read? Luke 10:26

- Which is easier to say, 'Your sins are forgiven you,' or to say, ' Rise and walk?' Luke 5:23
- What do you want me to do for you? Luke 18:41
- Who do you say that I am? Luke 9:20
- Woman, where are they? Has no one condemned you? John 8:10
- Show me a coin. Whose likeness and inscription has it? Luke 20:24
- Which of these three, do you think, proved neighbor to the man? Luke 10:36
- I ask you, is it lawful on the Sabbath to do good or to do harm, to save life or to destroy it? Luke 6:9

It's interesting that Jesus already knew the answers to the questions He was asking. So why ask them? He didn't ask them to find out information; He asked them to start conversations with people. He asked questions because He was genuinely interested in people. By asking powerful questions, Jesus empowered people to think through their opinions and what was happening around them. In the process, most of them came to a realization of the Truth.

> Great conversations are built on powerful questions.

The best questions are "open" questions. An open question doesn't have a specific answer, or a yes or no answer. Instead, it requires thought and allows our friend to answer however they want or need to. A "closed" question has a specific answer or can be answered with a yes or no. For example, "Did you have a good day today?" is a closed question. They will probably answer "Yes," "No," or "Sort of," and the conversation will be at a standstill until you ask another question. You can get a better conversation going, and ask about the same thing, by saying, "What was your day like today? What happened? How did it make you feel?" A lot of great open questions begin with the words "what" or "Can you tell me abo ut..." The more open questions you ask, the more your friend will begin to open up and share what they are thinking and feeling deep inside.[8] That's a foundation for a great relationship!

Great conversations are propelled forward by listening and responding. If you're going to ask a question, be sure to listen closely to the answer. This seems like a contradiction, because we want to *tell* people about Jesus, but it's much more important to listen than to talk.[9] When you listen, you communicate that you care. When you fail to listen, become distracted, or change the subject because you weren't paying attention, you communicate a lack of respect. Listening demonstrates humility and gentleness, two character qualities that Jesus embodied and told us to take upon ourselves (Matthew 11:29). Listening with a humble spirit creates trust and partnership.[10] Additionally, listening intently can give us clues to what's really happening in a person's heart, and help us ask questions that dive deeper into their true feelings and emotions. A person's tone of voice, the words they choose to stress in a sentence, and the emotion or mood they convey are all clues that can lead to further questions or can help you build a bridge to a stronger relationship. This is called *active listening*.

Active listening can tell us things that our friends are having a hard time saying, help us respond to their needs, or ask the right question to explore the situation further. Are they overwhelmed? Are they sad? Do they really need someone to talk to? I remember a woman who didn't seem to like me very much. She wasn't very nice to me, and I got the idea that she didn't think much of me. Life was really overwhelming her. She had three kids (a teenage girl, a pre-teen girl, and a younger boy). Both she and her husband were working to make ends meet, and they were in the middle of a home remodel. We were sitting in a meeting together when she expressed her exasperation with life. A major point of tension was her

It's much more important to listen than to talk.

home remodel. Her house had been torn apart for a few weeks, and progress didn't seem to be happening. She was tired of living in a construction zone. She was saying that she was exhausted, but it's what she wasn't saying that made the difference—she needed help! I heard it in her voice, and I saw it on her face. She wasn't my biggest fan, but that didn't matter. She needed help. I went to their house that Saturday and helped them with their project for about 8 hours. I still remember coughing from installing the insulation without proper breathing protection. But that investment of time instantly changed how she viewed me. She quickly became open to deeper and more meaningful conversations. To this day, I remain good friends with her and her family, and all because I listened and was able to help with some of the root of her frustration.

Active listening also means you can reflect back what you've heard. If you're listening well, you can affirm it by saying what you've just heard back to the person who said it. You can say things like, "So what your saying is..." or "Wow, I can't believe that..." or "What I'm hearing you say is . . . ". That will communicate to your conversation partner that you're really invested in what they're saying. It's not important that you agree with what your friend is saying, it's important that you're listening well. When you're talking to a friend and she brings up a topic that really seems to interest her, ask her a question about it. Remember, people love talking about themselves! So if they get excited, ask another question on that topic. One tip is to remember the five W's: Who? What? Where? When? and Why?[11] Exploring issues by asking those questions can really help you get a grasp of what your friend is feeling, and can help you keep the conversation going.

The Long Haul

Ultimately the goal is not just to have a great conversation, or to develop a great relationship, but to connect people to Jesus through relationship and conversation. That means we have to be in it for the long haul! Conversations take time, and it may take many conversations before someone is ready to respond to Jesus. Oftentimes our friends may see our point of view a little bit at a time, but eventually they will decide if they're all in. When that happens, it's likely we will see a complete surrender to Jesus, but in the meantime, there may be a necessary tension in our conversations. The tension is between who we are (disciples of Jesus Christ) and what we project (hopefully the love of God), and the way our friends view life and eternity. Brad Kallenberg describes it like this, "It is likely that I will see no progress in the conversation apart from a growing tension—even irritability—on the part of my friend...Now the question is whether I am willing to endure, even augment, this tension...Typically, I become discouraged by the mounting tension and foolishly move on to 'riper fruit' at just about the time 'the light dawns over the whole.'"[12] Don't give up just because you aren't seeing movement towards the cross. Stay in it for the long haul!

Having conversations that lead to relationship means more than just talking; it means doing life together. The conversations included in the second part of this book are not meant to be isolated discussions, but are instead designed to build upon one another, leading to the moment of tension when our friend decides whether or not they will follow Jesus. The tension in our conversations is relieved when we become complete friends, doing things together like friends do. That's why Chapter Seven asks the question, "What do you like to do?" Developing a relationship means doing the things your friends like to do. Having a conversation that leads to Jesus will most likely occur when you engage your friends in their passions and have fun together. Are you prepared to carry on conversations over the long haul? Are you so passionate about seeing your friends come to Jesus that you are willing to walk with them for a few years before progress is made? That's the long haul, and if you walk with them long enough, they will come to a point of decision.

Practice Makes Perfect

Now you've read all about having a great conversation and you're ready to try it. You definitely should! But one note of caution—don't expect to be an excellent conversationalist right away. In fact, it may take weeks, months, or even years of practice before you find yourself capable of carrying on the kind of conversation that can lead to Jesus. Most of us are trained to be self-centered from childhood, or we're very goal oriented so we're all about the message, and it can take time to learn to have others-centered conversations. Remember, practice makes perfect, so don't be afraid to try. Practice by asking different kinds of questions and seeing what produces the best responses. Practice listening for emotion, tone, and the way words are emphasized in a sentence and follow up on those clues with a question. Don't give up on having conversations that lead to Jesus just because you fail once, twice, or even thirty times. Conversations work, but it also requires *work* to become good at them. Having a great conversation is a skill, and just like so many skills, we have to keep practicing to get better at it. Make a goal to have one meaningful conversation every day, and try to get better at it each time.

Make a goal to have one meaningful conversation every day, and try to get better at it each time.

---

[1] Poe, 27.
[2] Joseph Umidi, "Foundations for Ministry Coaching," Lecture, Regent University, March 2, 2011.
[3] McRaney, The Art of Personal Evangelism, 101.
[4] Mark Petterson, "Strategic Conversations" in *HIS Guide to Evangelism* (Downers Grove: InterVarsity Press, 1977), 45.
[5] Robert T. Oliver, *Conversation: The Development and Expression of Personality* (Springfield, IL: Charles C. Thomas, 1961), 109-110.
[6] Green, *One to One,* 34.
[7] Tony Stoltzfus, Leadership Coaching: The Disciplines, Skills, and Heart of a Christian Coach (BookSurge Publishing, 2005).
[8] Comiskey et al., You Can Coach: How to Help Leaders Build Healthy Churches Through Coaching (Moreno Valley, CA: CCS Publishing, 2010), 39.
[9] Matthew Paul Turner, The Coffeehouse Gospel: Sharing Your Faith in Everyday Conversation (Marys Lake, FL: Relevant Books, 2004), 103.
[10] William Carr Peel and Walt Larimore, *Going Public with Your Faith: Becoming a Spiritual Influence at Work* (Grand Rapids: Zondervan, 2003), 69.
[11] Floyd Schneider, *Evangelism for the Fainthearted* (Grand Rapids: Kregel Publications, 2000), 56.
[12] Brad J. Kallenberg, *Live to Tell: Evangelism for a Postmodern Age* (Grand Rapids: Brazos Press, 2002), 61-62.

PART TWO
CONVERSATIONS

SIX
THE FIRST CONVERSATION:
WHAT'S YOUR STORY?

A few years ago I was running a youth retreat and we had a guest speaker named Craig. Craig was a pastor from a neighboring church, and I didn't know him all that well because he was a last minute pick. Honestly, I had waited too long to book the speaker, and when I called a respected friend for a recommendation he gave me Craig's name. Up until that point, I only knew Craig as a casual acquaintance. We knew each other because we were both pastors in the same denomination and in the same region. I trusted my friend's recommendation, so I booked Craig to come speak for us. I'll never forget that retreat or the time Craig and I got to spend together, but it had little to do with Craig's preaching. Don't get me wrong, his speaking was good, but that's not what I remember him for. I remember Craig because he was interested in me. After one of the services, Craig came up to me and started talking to me. He didn't ask me questions that focused on him, or about what was happening next; he only asked about me. Not only that, but after I started answering his questions I noticed how very interested he was in what I had to say. I didn't even think I was talking about anything interesting, but I had his enthusiastic interest. It made me feel valued, important, as though I mattered to someone. Has that ever happened to you?

Now let me tell you a different story. A few months ago I got to travel out of the country with several youth workers. It was a great trip! I love spending time with people who are passionate about the same things I am. Although I enjoyed my time with everyone, there was one person in particular on that trip I wanted to get to know. He was a pioneer in his field and a greatly respected leader, and I was looking forward to conversing with him and getting to know him better. I waited for an opportunity to speak with him naturally, and a few days into the trip I got my chance. We all stopped for lunch and I sat down at an empty space across from him. I began to talk with him by asking him some basic questions. I was interested to know more about him, and I was hoping that he would want to get to know me as well. To my disappointment, he didn't seem interested in talking to me. He politely answered my questions, but it was obvious I didn't have his interest. What made me feel even worse was that he didn't seem to be interested in getting to know me at all. The only thing he could talk about was himself. I walked away feeling dejected, unimportant, and devalued. Has this ever happened to you?

If you've ever spent time with anyone who can only talk about themselves, then you know how exhausting it can be! For a little while it seems interesting, but over time it really begins to wear out. Pretty soon you realize how very self-centered they are, and you begin to wonder if they would care if you ever saw each other again. On the other hand, if you've ever had the chance be around someone who was genuinely interested in you, then you know how good it feels to be heard. When someone wants to hear your story, your life becomes center stage and it brings value to your existence. It energizes you! Simply put, when someone takes an interest in you, it makes you feel fully human.

Loving By Listening

As Christians, we tend to want to start conversations about God by bringing up deep philosophical issues. We ask questions like, "Do you think God exists?" or "If you were to die today, do you know where you would go?" or "Do you think there's life after death?" The truth is we've likely been thinking about these questions since we became Christians. We're used to talking about them, and we assume everyone else will want to talk about them. But most people think more about themselves than they do about these issues. Most people would rather talk about themselves and be heard than to have a philosophical discussion about God and eternity.

In the early 1980's, it was reported that 72% of Americans thought about themselves "a good deal" of the time.[1] That was thirty years ago, but not a lot has changed in the decades since. It's part of our human nature to think about ourselves. Our problems consume us, our desires propel us forward, and our affections drive our actions and habits. Self-importance is a driving factor in the lives of Americans, and especially in the lives of teenagers. Not only do we spend time thinking about ourselves, we also have a desire to talk about ourselves. We need to be heard. In fact, the United Nations has even declared "The Right to be Heard" as one of the fundamental rights of children across the globe![2] To be heard is to be acknowledged; to be acknowledged is to be valued; to be valued is to be loved; to be loved is to be human.

To be heard is to be acknowledged;
to be acknowledged is to be valued;
to be valued is to be loved;
to be loved is to be human.

We don't need to look any further than Facebook, Twitter, and Instagram to know that people like to talk about themselves; they want to be heard and they want to be seen. Take a few moments to look through your Facebook or Instagram feed. How many postings are about the person posting them, or about something that is happening in their lives? How many "selfies" can you spot? One of the reasons social networks have become so popular is they create an easy platform for people to be heard and seen. If people need to be heard, and they are thinking about themselves so much, then that's a great place to start a conversation. Get them talking about themselves!

Ultimately, when someone is looking to be heard, they're looking to be loved. Loving people is what Christians do. That's part of our job as disciples of Jesus Christ. John wrote, "Love is from God, and whoever loves has been born of God and knows God. Anyone who does not love does not know God, because God is Love" (1 John 4:7-8 ESV). We must love the people God puts into our lives, and it's probably impossible to love someone without getting

> Loving people is what Christians do.

to know them. As Scott Jones said, "Loving a person well means knowing as much as possible about that person."[3] If you want to love a person, start by listening to their story!

Listen and Love First. Speak Second.

By listening to someone else's story you can find out a lot about them! We have a tendency, especially when we are young, to think that a lot of people approach life from the same perspective we do. If you talk to enough people, you will quickly realize there are many perspectives in the world radically different from ours! When I was in 6th grade there was a student in my class who struggled to make friends. He was an outcast who sat at a lunch table alone, dressed a little differently from everyone else, and was generally looked down upon. I was a Christian and wanted to be friends with him, and I thought there would be no better way of making friends than to tell him about Jesus. But he didn't want to hear about Jesus. He was an atheist. He didn't believe God existed, and so he wasn't ready to have a conversation about turning his life over to Jesus.

I wish I had taken the time to hear his story before I started to share the good news of the Gospel with him. Instead of listening to him, I insisted that Jesus was the answer to life's problems, and that he needed to turn his life over to Christ in order for everything to be better. Make no mistake; I still believe that Jesus is *the* answer, just as I did then, but that doesn't change the fact that he wasn't ready to hear it. If I'd taken the time to hear his heart, I would've realized that, in addition to Jesus, what he really needed was a friend. It turns out his parents had abandoned him, and he was forced to live with his alcoholic grandparents. They were poor, and most of the time he didn't get to do the things that most kids got to do. His clothes were all hand-me-downs or came from the thrift shop. Instead of being loved at home, he was treated as an unwanted inconvenience. He didn't know love, and so he could not believe that God existed. At the time, I had no idea anyone could believe anything other than God's existence. I knew love at home, so it was easy for me to accept that a God of love was real. I had heard of atheists, but I had never met one.

Instead of approaching him with something he felt he needed, I was offering him something he wasn't ready to consider. I was eager and excited to share about Jesus, but I wasn't ready to hear his story. I was ready to tell him all about God's love, but I wasn't ready to love him myself. And I definitely wasn't prepared to talk to somebody with such a different view of life from my own. Instead of a heartfelt talk about eternity, we ended up arguing. It wasn't a good encounter. If I had only taken the time to hear his story first, things may have ended up differently. I would have understood where he was coming from; his needs, his hurts, and his desires. A friendship would likely have been born out of that conversation. Instead, I charged in recklessly, trying to express a Gospel based in love without actually loving.

I made several mistakes in that encounter, but mostly I made the mistake of not listening or loving before speaking. If I'd done that, I would've realized how different his perspective was from mine. The truth is, most people are vastly different from us and we must approach every person based on their own perspective. Michael Green put it like this:

> People are so varied, and their interests, starting points, and needs are so diverse, that it is asking for trouble to barge in with some premeditated sermonette or some technique learned from a book about the best way to approach people. After all, we are individuals, and we do not appreciate being treated as if we were just some simple human specimens, ripe to be evangelized![4]

If you want to know what someone's perspective is, ask them about their story! Only then will you know if they came from an abused home, or what their family was like, or their values, or what they think about life.

Scott Jones compares Christians who want to share their faith with a salesmen who want to sell a product. A good salesman learns something about his customer. In fact, a lot of retailers pay good money to discover how to market their product to consumers. Retailers like Apple or internet companies like Facebook know the average age, income, and level of education of their customers. They know what products will sell best in different parts of the country. Jones asks, "Why is it that Christians do not study non-Christians with the same vigor as salespeople? If we are truly motivated by love and want to love others well, we need to be even better informed than those whose motives are less lofty."[5] Now please don't think the Gospel is a product to sell, like an iPhone! The Gospel is so much more than this, but the principle here is the same. You probably need to get to know someone in order to adequately share Jesus with them!

Story is Truth

For my atheist classmate, it didn't really matter that I wanted to share the "Truth" of the Gospel with him. In fact, he didn't find it to be truthful at all. His life taught him that love was non-existent, and so a God of love could not be true. His story was his truth. His life experience outweighed any facts or scriptures I could share with him. This is the heart of what social scientists have called "postmodernism." The central thought of postmodernism could be stated like this, "Just because the Gospel is true for you, that doesn't mean it's true for me. And if it's not true for me, it's not Truth." In our world today, fact is not as important as experience. Experience determines what truth is.

This may sound different from what you've always been told, but think about it in terms of pizza. Imagine there is a pizza shop in your town that it is known to have the best pizza around. Every food critic says this pizza shop is the best, and it's always ranked at the top of every list of pizza shops. In your town, it's an accepted fact that this pizza shop is number one!

Now imagine you go there for the first time expecting the greatest slice of pizza. It comes out steaming hot, dripping with cheese and covered with your favorite toppings, and you can't wait to bite into it. Then something you didn't expect happens—you take a bite and it tastes like a heaping mound of hot garbage! Gross! How could this happen?! Everyone said this is the best pizza shop, but your taste buds are telling you this is not true. Clearly, the pizza shop down the block is better, because you've had their pizza and it tasted great. Your experience is telling you something other than the accepted truth. And you probably won't come back to this pizza shop again! Your experience is your story. And your story is your truth.

> In our world today, fact is not as important as experience.

The same is true with everyone else. Their life experience is their story, and their story is their truth. Did you know that Jesus was a great storyteller? It's true! He loved to tell stories. The stories he told are called parables, and the Gospels contain 32 of them. Most of them are recorded in the Book of Luke, but Matthew and Mark contain some as well. Jesus often told stories that were tied to real life experiences, like the parable of the weeds (Matthew 13:24-40), or the parable of the Wedding Feast (Luke 14:7-11). Jesus used everyday experiences to communicate eternal Truth, because he knew that our experiences determine what we accept as being true.

In addition, by telling stories based in real life, he also taught us that eternal truth *can be found* in our life experiences. When you listen to someone else's story, you can hear their truth about life, and perhaps their truth about God. Not only that, but you can probably pick up on the traces of God's story intermingled with theirs. Jesus told us God draws men to himself (John 6:44), and the Holy Spirit is at work convicting the world of sin, righteousness, and judgment (John 16:8). That means God is already trying to communicate with those who do not know Him. When you take the time to listen to someone's story, there's a very good chance you'll be able to discover at least one area where God is trying to communicate with them.

> When you take the time to listen to someone else's story, there's a very good chance you'll be able to discover at least one area where God is trying to communicate to them.

At this point, it's not important if you consider their truth to be accurate. What's important is that you're listening! You are discovering what their version of the truth is. You are discovering their perspective, their hurts, their dreams, their stories. You don't have to agree to listen. When you listen to their version of the truth, you communicate that they matter to you without saying a word. That is powerful!

> When you listen to their version of the truth, you communicate that they matter to you without saying a word.

Jesus is Our Example

If you doubt the importance of hearing someone's story, then you need to think about Jesus' life. John 1:1-4 says that Jesus is God, that He's been around since the beginning of time, that everything was made by Him, and that "the life that was the light of men" was in Him. Then in verse 14, John says that Jesus "became flesh and dwelt among us" (ESV). In other words, Jesus left Heaven and came to man on earth. John was a good Hebrew, and when he uses the word "dwelt" to describe Jesus coming to earth, he used it purposefully. In fact, it's a rare word that only John uses in the New Testament, and the only other place it's found is in the Book of Revelation. The word "dwelt" in the original Greek language literally means "to tabernacle" or "to tent."[6] John is referring to the time in the Hebrew history when God's presence was found in the tabernacle, or the big tent, in the middle of the Israelite camp in the wilderness.

Have you ever gone camping in the wilderness with a group of people? Or have you every camped in a place with a lot of other tents? What if God came into the campground and pitched his own tent just down the row from yours? That's the picture that John is painting when he says Jesus "dwelt" among us. God created the heavens and the earth, made everything that we see, lived in heaven, but chose to come to the earth and pitch his tent alongside ours. He came to us. He experienced the story of man. He learned the truth as man saw it. He came to earth and got to know us. He learned our stories. If we are going to be fully formed disciples of Christ, we must do the same thing. If there's someone you want to share the Gospel with, go to them and dwell among them by learning their story.

> Jesus came to earth and got to know us. He learned our stories.

Having the Conversation

Now it's time to start learning other people's stories—it's time to start some conversations! Every good conversation begins and flows with good questions. Here are some questions to get you going, but you can always develop your own and allow the conversation to flow naturally:

- ***How's life treating you?*** Start with something simple. When they give you a response, go deeper. If they said, *"Not Good,"* reply by saying *"I'm sorry to hear that. Tell me about it."* If they say *"Great,"* reply by saying *"Awesome! Tell me about it, what makes it so great?"*
- ***Tell me about your family.*** This is not a question, but an invitation, which is just as good. Finding out about someone's family is so important. Some follow up questions could be: *What does your dad do for a living? What does your mom do? What are your siblings like? What's a night like in your house? What are some of your favorite family traditions?*
- ***Where did you grow up?*** Everyone grew up somewhere. Knowing this can be a key to finding out about someone's past. When something interests you, or when you can tell something is interesting to them, follow up by asking something like, "*What was that like?"*
- **What gets you excited?** This question deals with someone's passions. It's a great conversation starter! Another way to put it is, *"What are you passionate about?"* Follow up with, *"Tell me more"* or *"What is it that you love about it?"*
- ***Who are your favorite people?*** Find out who your friend finds to be inspirational. Then ask, *"What is it about them that you enjoy so much?"* You can learn a lot about what they look up to in this way.
- ***What's your favorite thing to talk about?*** There's no better way to get them talking than by focusing on their favorite discussion topic. Continue the conversation by saying "*Tell me about that. What makes it your favorite thing?"*

- ***What's the most significant part of your childhood?*** This can unlock a lot of emotion and life history. Follow up with, *"What made it significant?"*
- ***What's the most important part of your life now?*** Get real with them, and find out what's important currently. Ask *"What makes it so important?"*

Once you meet someone, you can create opportunities to have better conversations and really explore his or her life through the questions above. Invite him to the mall, or for a cup of coffee, or to McDonalds. If you're hanging out with a bunch of friends from church, invite the person you want to reach along. Send him a birthday card, or a get-well card when he's sick. You can always use your common experiences to start a conversation, as well. If something interesting happens and you both experience it, just ask *"What did you think about that?"*

You can always use your common experiences to start a conversation.

Connecting to the Gospel

Finding out someone's story is one of the easiest ways to connect people to Jesus. Why? Because it's likely they will want to know your story! Even those people who never ask about your life will eventually break down and want to know more about you, or at least about why you're curious about them. I've lived in my current house for about 10 years. For 10 years I've had the same set of neighbors across the street. I pray for my neighbors, and I desire so intensely for them to know Jesus, because I know they are currently distant from the Lord. I've also been praying for opportunities to connect them to God through conversation. However, it's been difficult to connect with them because we live on a busy road, and they tend to be secluded.

One day this past winter we got around 10" of snow and everybody in the neighborhood was home because the roads were too dangerous to drive on. I had just finished clearing my driveway when I saw them out working to clear theirs. I knew this would be a great opportunity to demonstrate God's love through action. As we worked alongside each other I asked, "So what do you do for living?" They replied and I began to go deeper with the conversation. "What got you started doing that?" "How interesting! Tell me more about it." Eventually, they asked me about what I did. I replied, "I travel all around the state and help students start Bible Clubs in their school, share their faith with their friends, and I help churches do the same thing." They answered, "That's great! When I was a teenager I was involved in something like a Bible Club at my school. I even went on a retreat one time." Immediately the connecting point for the Gospel was discovered. It had been there all along, but it wasn't until I was able to share some of my story that it became exposed.

The key to connecting our friends to the Gospel through our story is an authentic experience with God. In other words, we have to be able to share how our experience with God has changed our life and made it meaningful. Our story shapes us, and the story of the Gospel needs to be what shapes us ultimately. If we can't talk about how the Gospel has shaped our lives, we will have difficulty in proclaiming the Gospel to be true.[7] However, when we can tell stories of God authentically out of our own experience, people will respond, for we will have given them the truth.[8] Just as our friends' stories and experiences determine their truth, so our stories and experiences determine our truth. In other words, the stories we tell about Jesus changing our lives are absolutely true, because they are true to us. Our experience tells us so!

The key to connecting our friends to the Gospel through our story is an authentic experience with God.

A lot of people may have a difficult time believing the Bible, or accepting the word of the church or a preacher. But most people will respect your personal stories, feelings, and experiences. Stories are real. Stories are memorable. Stories leave an impression of personal truth. Your story tells others about God's power at work in your life. It's not an explanation of how Jesus saves us, or even a plea for salvation. But it does demonstrate an experience of God in your life—a God-story! A God-story is a personal truth that cannot be taken away from you. Have you ever felt a great sense of peace from God? That's a God-story! Have you been healed, or has someone in your family been healed? That's a God-story! Do you turn to God in prayer when you're worried about something? That's a God-story!

A few years ago I was in Ukraine helping with a Bible Study at a Christian-based English language study club. There were many around the table who were doubtful about God's existence. Ukraine is a former communist country, and in the days of communism it was thought to be foolishness to believe in God. The Bible study focused on Hezekiah, and how God prolonged his life (2 Kings 20). The conversation turned to questions about the end of life, God's healing power, and His timing. Through a translator, I shared the following story about my wife's father:

> Shortly after we were married my father-in-law was diagnosed with cancer and was told he had just a few years to live. After a few years of fighting the cancer through surgery, medicine, and natural remedies, things began to take a turn for the worse. He was given just a few days to live and placed in the care of health professionals who would help him to die in peace. Around that same time another of his daughters was engaged and soon-to-be married. It didn't appear as though he would live long enough to walk her down the aisle. Then a curious thing happened—he started to get better. Miraculously, when every doctor said he was at death's door, he began to get stronger and put on weight. Soon he was discharged from

> terminal care and sent home. Not long after that he walked his daughter down the aisle at her wedding. Shortly thereafter, she became pregnant with what would be his first grandbaby. But that good news was soon shattered with bad news: the cancer had returned, and it was worse than ever. He now had only months to live. God had healed him, but it was only temporary. As his life faded slowly over the length of his daughter's pregnancy, he fought to hang on. He hung on long enough to hold his first grandchild in the delivery room, and died six days later. Some would say that it was just a coincidence that he got better when he did. But I am convinced that, like Hezekiah, God extended his life for a year and a half so that he could experience some of the greatest joys on earth: walking his daughter down the aisle and holding his first grandbaby.

I shared most of that with my head down, not able to make eye contact, I was fighting tears of emotion as I shared this God-story. When I was finished I looked up to discover everyone in the room had tears in their eyes, and some were even weeping. Walls of unbelief began to break down as everyone recognized the Truth in my God-story. I could not prove that it was true by scientific fact, but I didn't need to. My authentic experience did the work. Your God-stories will do the same!

Just as our friends' stories and experiences determine their truth, so our stories and experiences determine our truth.

Finding Your Story

Your story is the testimony of how God touched your life. But it can also be smaller stories of how God has worked in you or around you. Your testimony of God's work in your life is powerful. In Revelation 12, a story is told about a war in heaven between the angels and Satan, who is called the "accuser of the brethren." We are the brethren. Verse 11 says Satan was conquered "by the blood of the Lamb, and the word of their (the brethren's) testimony." The two most powerful things in Satan's ultimate defeat are (1) the Blood of the Lamb—Jesus sacrifice on the cross, and (2) the word of our testimony—when we share what God has done for us. This is simply amazing! Did you know there was so much power in your story?

Shaping your testimony is easier than you think. In his book, *The Coffeehouse Gospel*, Matthew Paul Turner offers the following questions to help you discover your own story:[9]

1. What was your childhood like? Were you a churchgoer? Was a life in Jesus something you pursued? If not, did you believe in anything remotely spiritual?
2. When was the first time you remember hearing about God, Jesus, or the Christian faith? How old were you?
3. What was your immediate response to the Gospel?
4. If you grew up knowing Jesus, was there a time that you remember it really clicking? Can you explain this turn of events?
5. If you resisted your first hearing the Gospel message, what is the main reason you didn't believe at first?
6. What ultimately changed your heart toward the Gospel message?
7. Where there any life occurrences—a death in the family, illness, a miracle, a new relationship, etc.—that stood out as landmarks to you on your journey of faith?
8. How did God use these life landmarks to pull you into a relationship with Him?
9. What attracted you to know more about Jesus? What part of your relationship with Him has influenced you the most?
10. What about your life changed after you made your decision to be a Jesus follower?

Answer these questions thoughtfully, then begin to write out your story.

It's not necessary for you to always share your full testimony, however. In fact, often it's more natural just to share one brief story about how God worked in your life. This is a God-story. William Peel and Walt Larimore give a few tips for developing your own stories about your faith in God, and how they've impacted your life. They write:[10]

- Make a list of the times when you had a meaningful encounter with God. It may have been a time:
  - When God did something meaningful or significant in your life
  - When you enjoyed and experienced pleasure in your relationship with God
  - When you experienced intimacy or renewal in your relationship with God
  - When God spoke clearly to you or gave you guidance
  - When God worked through you to accomplish His purposes
- Choose one or two of these experiences and write a brief faith story about each

When you've got some God-stories down, practice them! Ask a Christian friend if you can share them. Ask your pastor if you can give your testimony or story in church or youth group. Above all else, look for opportunities to share your story as you listen to the stories of others. Don't force it! Wait for the invitation from your friend or a nudging from the Holy Spirit.

Praying

When you get to know someone better, put that information to use by praying for them. Knowing their life story, their hurts, dreams, passions, and desires should drive you to have a greater compassion for them. Do they have a need? Take it to the Lord in prayer. When you pray for them, be open for insight from the Holy Spirit. God will speak to you and give you even greater ways to connect to them. If it's appropriate, you can even ask them if you can pray for them, or let them know that you care about them and that you're asking God to help them. Love them genuinely by listening to them, then praying sincerely for them. If you don't have anyone to have a conversation with yet, pray that God would send you that opportunity. Everyone has a story. Everyone's story needs to be heard. You can be more powerful by listening to someone else's story than you could ever imagine.

---

[1] Daniel Yankelovich, New Rules: Searching for Self-Fulfillment in a World Turned Upside Down (New York: Random House, 1981), 5.
[2] Gerison Lansdown, *Every Child's Right To Be Heard* (London: Save the Children UK, 2011), Adobe PDF eBook.
[3] Jones, 126.
[4] Green, *One to One,* 23.
[5] Jones, 126.
[6] Andreas J. Köstenberger, "John," in *John, Acts,* vol. 2 of *Zondervan Illustrated Bible Backgrounds Commentary: New Testament.* ed. Clinton E. Arnold; Accordance electronic ed. (Grand Rapids: Zondervan, 2002), 10.
[7] Kallenberg, 37.
[8] Rick Richardson, Evangelism Outside the Box: New Ways to Help People Experience the Good News (Downers Grove, Ill: Intervarsity Press, 2000), 93.
[9] Turner, 96-97.
[10] Peel and Larimore, 96.

SEVEN
THE SECOND CONVERSATION:
WHAT DO YOU LIKE TO DO?

I grew up in church, but it wasn't until I was in tenth grade that I decidedly committed by life to Jesus. Ninth grade had been a difficult year for me, as I made friends whom I allowed to influence me in a negative way. I was sneaking out of my house late at night, going to parties, smoking, and experimenting with drugs and alcohol. Sometimes I feel like I'm lucky to have survived my ninth grade year! When God got hold of my life, I knew much of that had to change. God didn't just want part of me, He wanted all of me. One of the challenges of making that change was finding someone who could be a positive influence, a Christian friend, in my life. That's when Jason made a remarkable impact on me.

Jason and I had known each other for a long time. It seemed like our paths had crossed pretty regularly since childhood, and Jason was an active member of the youth group I began attending when I fully committed myself to Christ. Until that time we had only been acquaintances, but soon Jason began to hang out with me. I really didn't have Christian friends, and that was part of the struggle with my belief in God. It can be hard to believe when you feel like you don't belong! It wasn't long until he was asking about what I liked to do. Soon we discovered that we had a common interest—cars! He had an early 1980's Ford Mustang, and I had a 1989 Ford Taurus. I told him that I had never changed the oil in a car, but I wanted to learn. He told me it was easy, and that he would show me! Soon I was at his house, driving my car up onto ramps, climbing under the engine beside Jason, and learning how to change my oil. The spark plugs were next! Soon we discovered another common interest—we liked to build models. I liked to build model ships and airplanes, and Jason liked to build model cars. Jason invited me over to build models one Friday night. We sat in his basement with our model kits, glue, and paint, and had a great conversation about life, girls, cars, and Jesus. Those times we spent together, doing what I liked to do, made a huge difference in my commitment to God!

> It can be hard to believe when you feel like you don't belong.

I know working on cars and building models may seem like simple hobbies that are not connected to sharing Jesus, but through our common interests God used Jason to change my life. And it all started with the question, "So what do you like to do?" By taking an interest in what I liked to do, Jason was making it possible for me to belong. Because I felt like I belonged, it was easier for me to believe. Jason was willing to meet me on my level. He communicated with me in language that I understood—my interests! And Jason showed genuine love when he chose to engage in my interests with me. Do you have someone in mind that you want to share Jesus with? Have you asked them about their hobbies, interests, and passions? Sharing the things people like to do are great bridges that span across unbelief and put us on firm footing to share the Gospel.

I know what you're thinking: Can this really work? Can a mundane, every day hobby or interest lead someone to Jesus? Can someone's interest in cars, or video games, or makeup, or fashion be used to bring them into connection with the creator of the universe? Of course it can! It may seem silly to you on the surface. But it works! I recently emailed around 800 students who are committed to live as missionaries on their high school campuses and asked them, "What are you believing God for?" One of my favorite responses from that brief survey was Allison, a high school senior. She wrote, "I am believing that God can take the itty bitty mundane parts of my life and make something beautiful for His kingdom out of it." When we talk about these seemingly mundane things, it tells the person we're talking to that we care about them, even in the little things.[1] It also communicates that God is interested in the little things because we are Christ's ambassadors! Doesn't serving a God who is interested in the details of our lives seem better than a God who doesn't care about our interests?

> Sharing the things people like to do are great bridges that span across unbelief and put us on firm footing to share the Gospel.

Interests and Identities

Think for a second about some of the different groups of students in high school—sports teams, the band, the national honor society, the drama students, etc. Have you ever noticed that a lot of these groups, or more specifically the people in these groups, get labeled with nicknames that are tied to their interests? Some of these labels are good, and some are discouraging. For example, students who play sports may be labeled "jocks," while students who are in the marching band get labeled as "band geeks." Students who are good at school and learning are probably labeled as "nerds" or "brainiacs." The list goes on and on—preps, scene kids, rich kids, choir kids, loners, skaters, hipsters, mean girls, thespians. While some of these nicknames don't sound complimentary, it's fairly normal for a lot of students to proudly take on the nickname of their interest group. In my high school the marching band students were proud to be labeled "band geeks" and created their own culture around it. They loved being in band and playing music together, so they embraced an identity that was tied to what they loved. Our interests are often tied to our identities, and our identities are often tied to personal fulfillment.

Having an identity and feeling personally fulfilled are two of the biggest needs Americans have. One of the largest churches in the United States is Willow Creek Community Church. When they began in 1975, they studied and developed a profile of the "unchurched" in society. They found that personal fulfillment was the top felt need of people who are apart from God, and identity was the second.[2] By learning what people like to do, you are on the path to discovering two crucial needs in the lives of people: what they do for personal fulfillment, and where they find their identity. When we dive into the interests of others, we're not just being curious, we are meeting their needs.

> Our interests are often tied to our identities, and our identities are often tied to personal fulfillment.

Common Ground

When you find out what your friend likes to do, you may find out that you have common interests. I have a neighbor I pray for on a regular basis. She doesn't really have a religious foundation in her life. Her grandmother was Catholic, but that is about as far as her religious experience goes. I get to see this neighbor often, and when I do I try to have the best conversation I can with her. It wasn't long after she moved in that we discovered we have common interests. First and foremost, she is an animal lover! She has a dog, a few cats, and fosters dogs for a local animal shelter often. My wife and I love animals too. We have two Great Danes and would probably have more if we could handle it! Not only do we share a love of animals in common, but we also love the outdoors. She is an avid runner, hiker, and enjoys camping. While my wife and I don't like running, we do enjoy hiking and camping. I never have to worry about what I will talk about when I see my neighbor. When I discovered her interests, I discovered we had a lot in common. I don't need to build a bridge to have a conversation with her, because we already share common ground. As Michael Green stated, "The interest we share *is* the bridge: we hardly need to do any building."[3]

Not only can finding out what people like to do help you find common ground, but you can also detect the ways that God may be speaking to them. Earlier I wrote that God is constantly drawing people to Himself, and that the Holy Spirit is always at work convicting the world of sin, righteousness, and judgment. What if we could detect God working in someone by discovering their hobbies and interests? When it comes to my neighbor, there is a clear path that God is using to draw her to himself—from animals to the outdoors—she loves God's creation! She hasn't yet surrendered herself to the Creator of all things, but her deep love and compassion for God's creatures and his created world are unmistakable. In a sense, she is already in obedience to God's Word by taking care of the parts of creation that come into her life. I am praying that this common ground of God's Spirit at work, combined with our common interest and our continued conversations, will provide the opportunity to share faith with her. When it happens, I believe it will be eye opening!

What if we could detect God working in someone by discovering their hobbies and interests?

The Apostle Paul was a master at finding hints of God's Spirit at work in the lives of those he ministered to. Acts 17 contains the story of his visit to Athens and to the Areopagus, also called Mars' Hill. The Areopagus was a giant rock, rising 377 feet into the air, which means it was one of the most recognizable landmarks in Paul's day.[4] There on Mars' Hill, Paul gave a speech that embraced the interests of the Athenians and pointed out God's work among them. Descended from the Greek culture of worshipping many gods, the people of Athens had shrines, statues, and objects to help them worship as many gods as possible. Not only that, but they didn't want to upset any of the gods by ignoring them, so they also had an altar with an inscription to an "unknown" god.[5] Paul recognized their interest in religion and spirituality, and used the "unknown god" as an opportunity to share Jesus.

He said, "As I passed along and observed the objects of your worship, I found also an altar with this inscription, 'To the unknown god.' What therefore you worship as unknown, this I proclaim to you. The God who made the world and everything in it, being Lord of heaven and earth, does not live in temples made by man, nor is he served by human hands, as though he needed anything, since he himself gives to all mankind life and breath and everything" (vv 23–25 ESV). Paul went on to quote some of the Athenians own religious poets, who had written about the "unknown god," saying "In Him we live and move and have our being" and "We are indeed His offspring" (vs 28). Paul dove into the Athenians' lives, habits, and interests and recognized how the Holy Spirit had already been speaking to them, even though they hadn't realized it. He connected with them by using their language, culture, and styles of communication, all the while affirming they were on the right path, just a little misguided.[6]

By discovering what the people of Athens "liked to do" and engaging them where they were, Paul was quickly able to gain their respect and attention. By acknowledging that there was some legitimacy in their spiritual quest, he helped them feel like they belonged, which eventually led them to belief. The results were amazing! Scripture records that some of the people believed (vs 34), including a man named Dionysius and a woman named Damaris. Dionysius was a member of the local ruling council, a leader in his community who would go on to lead the church in Athens.[7] Damaris was probably a prostitute, a member of the class of women known as the Heitarai.[8] These women were foreigners, well educated, and were brought to Athens to keep wealthy men company.[9] After accepting faith in Christ, she likely played an important role in the church at Athens. Think about what would have happened if Paul hadn't embraced the Athenians' interests: the church in Athens would likely not have gotten started and a prostitute would not have been delivered from her life of bondage. It all happened because Paul stopped to observe Athenian culture, and their extreme interest in religion and spirituality. It's amazing what can happen when you take an interest in how other people live their lives; their hobbies, interests, and their passions!

Jesus is Our Example

Luke tells us about how Peter, James, and John came to be disciples of Jesus in chapter 5 of his gospel. The three men were fishermen on the Sea of Galilee, and had just finished an unsuccessful day of fishing. They were washing their fishing equipment, likely in frustration, while Jesus was teaching on the shoreline. When the crowed pressed into him, Jesus got into one of their boats and taught the crowd from the boat. When he was done teaching, Jesus went fishing with Peter, James, and John. What would it be like to fish with God? Imagine if Jesus found out what you liked to do, and then did it with you! Peter didn't think it was a good idea to fish at that time. After all, they had fished all night with no results. But Jesus took an interest in them and the result was a catch of fish so enormous that the fishing nets started breaking apart.

Peter soon realized that something was different about Jesus; He wasn't like all the other teachers of the day. What if God could use you like this? Could the Holy Spirit empower your interest in the hobbies of a friend to bring about a realization that Christ is the Son of God? One of the most remarkable parts of this story is that going fishing was Jesus' idea. Jesus knew that Peter, James, and John were fishermen. Fishing is what they liked to do, and Jesus created an opportunity to do it with them. Jesus took the first step. He sought out the people He wanted to impact, and by using their interest in fishing, He made them fishers of men.[10]

Jesus took the first step. He sought out the people He wanted to impact, and by using their interest in fishing, He made them fishers of men.

Belonging Before Believing

What do you think of when you hear the name "Saint

Patrick"? You're probably getting flashes of the color green, four-leaf clovers, leprechauns, and a pot of gold in your mind. Most of that has nothing to do with the real Saint Patrick! Saint Patrick came to Ireland in the 5th century and is credited with bringing Christianity to most of the country and parts of Scotland. George Hunter III researched Saint Patrick's methods for sharing the Gospel with the Celts, because the results of Saint Patrick's work are hard to be argued with: he baptized tens of thousands of people, planted about 700 churches, and ordained about 1,000 Irish (Celtic) priests. It's believed 30-40 of the 150 tribes in Ireland became Christian during his time.[11]

One of the powerful methods he used was to make potential believers feel like they were a part of the community. "The Celtic model for reaching people" was to first welcome those outside of the church into the church community.[12] They did not wait for people to be "saved" or to accept the message of the cross to welcome them into fellowship. Instead, they welcomed people in friendship, believing that as unbelievers experienced the genuine friendship and love of a Christ-like community, they would eventually come around to the realization of the truth of the Gospel. So Patrick and his fellow priests would set up their churches as close to the center of town as possible. They took an interest in the community and its people!

Patrick believed that if people could feel accepted, as though they belonged and had a common identity, then faith was just one step away. This is distinctly different from the current method that the church uses in the United States. Normally we invite people to accept the message of Jesus, and then we invite them into the fellowship of the church. But in Celtic society, as it is in many places in the world today, it was essential that the church be an open and welcoming society. As Jim Henderson put it, "The Celtic Christians treated outsiders like insiders."[13] Today it's important that people can "belong before they believe."[14] If you want to make people feel like they belong, take in an interest in what they like to do. Get involved in their lives!

If people can feel accepted, as though they belong and have a common identity, then faith is just one step away.

Geek Night

In a small high school in Central Pennsylvania several Christian students have committed themselves to being missionaries on their campus for the Gospel. A few months ago, four of them began to meet weekly to discuss and strategize how they could impact their school for Jesus. They prayed that God would help them identify another group of students in their school that they could share Jesus with, and they prayed that God would give them an idea of how to move forward. God answered their prayer in a special way! This particular school has a group of students who love to play online computer games, and who are also strong atheists, and it was this group of online-gaming-atheists whom God placed in the hearts of the missionaries. As they prayed and talked about what they could do to share the Gospel, they conceived of a weekly group-gaming night, accompanied by discussions on atheism, with the hope of eventually being able to share the Gospel. The missionaries wanted to engage in something the atheists liked to do—and so Geek Night was born!

Geek Night happens two Friday evenings each month when the gamers are invited to someone's house for a group online-gaming party. They all bring their computers and gaming consoles, and the missionaries provide food and fun. Many of these atheist students had previously decided that all religion was evil, and some even vowed to never set foot in a church. The missionaries took an interest in them, despite their differences, and the results have been incredible. Nearly 25 people attended the biggest Geek Night. Even better, a number of the atheists started attending church events, and even church services, as the missionaries invited them. At the time of this writing, several of the online-gamers have turned from atheism and accepted Jesus into their lives! All this happened because four Christian students took an interest in what some of their lost friends like to do, and then created an environment where they could belong before they believed. It's amazing what can happen when you take an interest in what people like to do!

Having the Conversation

Every good conversation begins and flows with good questions. Here are some questions to get you going, but you can always develop your own and allow the conversation to flow naturally:

- ***What do you like to do?*** Find out about their hobbies! Watch for them to get excited, and then dive deeper by saying *"Tell me more. What makes that so exciting for you?"*
- ***What are you interested in?*** This may not be the same as a hobby, so it's important to ask. A lot of people are

interested in history, but they don't "do" history. Still you can find out their interests and learn about them this way. Follow up with, *"What makes it so compelling?"*

- ***Could you show me that sometime?*** This is where the rubber really meets the road! Once you've learned what they like to do, engage them in it. Meet them where they are and do it with them. Other ways of asking this question are: *"Could I try that?"* or *"Would you teach me about that?"* or *"Could I come check that out sometime?"* or *"I really think that's interesting. How can I learn more?"* or *"Could we do that together?"*

Finding out what someone likes to do starts as a conversation, but it ultimately ends in action. You've got to walk with your friend and actually do that hobby, or engage that interest with them to progress the relationship. You need to do life with them! If they play a sport, watch their game and bring them some Gatorade, or find out if you can help them practice. If they like fishing, ask them to teach you how to fish. If they enjoy reading, read a book together and have a discussion on the book you've read.

At first this may seem forced or unauthentic. After all, if you aren't naturally interested in what they like to do, aren't you just pretending to be something you're not to get what you want? This is where your attitude is so important. If you really want to love them, then it's not unauthentic to learn about their interests, and it's not forced to try to engage in their hobbies with them. For example, I love Star Trek! I know some of you are laughing at that (haters gotta hate), but it's true. My wife isn't naturally a Star Trek fan, but because she genuinely loves me, she will watch hours of Star Trek with me. Let God's love for people drive you, enabling you to embrace interests and hobbies

Finding out what someone likes to do starts as a conversation, but it ultimately ends in action.

you never thought possible.

This is what the Apostle Paul did when he was on his missionary journeys. He wrote that he was "compelled" by the love of Christ, convinced in his heart that Jesus died for all mankind (2 Corinthians 5:14). In his first letter to the church at Corinth, he wrote, "I have become all things to all people so that by all possible means I might save some" (9:23). If Paul was with Jews, he took on Jewish interests. If he was with Gentiles, he lived and engaged the Gentiles on their terms. If someone was at a disadvantage, he shared that disadvantage. "Paul was saying that as a witness he recognized it was up to him to adapt to the unevangelized. The witness adjusts to those he seeks to win, not vice-versa."[15] Jesus became a fisherman! Paul became a Gentile! Some Christian students became geeks! What will you learn, become, or participate in so that you can share the Gospel? How will you make your friends belong so that they can find it easier to believe?

> What will you learn, become, or participate in so that you can share the Gospel?

Connecting to the Gospel

When you start to engage people in what they like to do, friendships grow stronger. When friendships grow stronger, the opportunities to connect people to God increase. One of the first ways to connect people to the Gospel is through conversation. When you begin to ask people about what they like to do, there's a good chance they'll ask you about what you like to do. I surely hope that, if you're reading this book, one of your top hobbies will be going to church or church activities, and that your deepest interests will be in God and His Word. If you love your church or youth group, or you love reading God's word or praying, why not talk about it? It would be the most authentic thing you could share! And if it's truly your interest, it will fit right into the conversation. Furthermore, as you talk about it, you're inviting your friend to respond to your interest in one way or another. As Rebecca Pippert writes, "It is far more winsome to toss out a few casual comments about your relationship to God or about your Bible study...and then see what happens."[16]

A second way of connecting people to the Gospel is by using the method of Saint Patrick. As you begin to take an interest in your friend by doing things together, it will become natural for you to invite them to a church activity, or to hang out with you and your Christian friends. You can invite them into an environment where they can feel like they belong, and that makes it so much easier for them to believe and have faith in God. And you don't have to do it alone. The best way to make someone feel like they belong is to surround them with people who care about them. To create a truly embracing culture of belonging, get some of your Christian friends to help you in this effort. Together, create an environment or an opportunity that engages what your lost friends like to do.

The best way to make someone feel like they belong is to surround them with people who care about them.

Praying

Ask God to help you become a better friend by taking an interest in your friends' hobbies and passions. Begin to pray that as you find out what your friends like to do, you would be able to see where the Holy Spirit has already been working, drawing them to God. Ask God to give you creative ideas and opportunities to create environments where your lost friends can belong, making it easier for them to believe. Everybody likes to do something, so get out there and use that interest for the Gospel!

---

[1] Jim Henderson, a.k.a. "LOST": Discovering Ways to Connect with the People Jesus Misses Most (Colorado Springs: WaterBrook Press, 2005), 56.
[2] G.A. Pritchard, Willow Creek Seeker Services: Evaluating a New Way of Doing Church (Grand Rapids: Baker Books, 1996), 70-71.
[3] Green, Sharing Your Faith with Friends and Family: Talking About Jesus Without Offending (Grand Rapids: Baker Books, 2005), 33.
[4] Hubert M. Martin, "Areopagus," in *Anchor Yale Bible Dictionary*, 1:370.
[5] "To An Unkown God," in *Fire Bible Notes*, Acts 17:23.
[6] Richardson, 78.
[7] F.F. Bruce, *The Book of the Acts*, New International Commentary on the New Testament. Accordance electronic ed. (Grand Rapids: Eerdmans, 1988), 343.
[8] William M. Ramsay, *St. Paul the Traveller and the Roman Citizen* (Grand Rapids: Baker Book House, 1985), 252.
[9] Ben Witherington, "Damaris," in *Anchor Yale Bible Dictionary*, 2:5.
[10] Stanley Skreslet, *Picturing Christian Witness: New Testament Images of Disciples in Mission* (Grand Rapids: William B. Eerdmans Publishing Company, 2006), 83.
[11] George Hunter III, *The Celtic Way of Evangelism* (Nashville: Abingdon Press, 2000), 23.
[12] Ibid, 53.
[13] Henderson, 54.
[14] Hunter, 55.
[15] Peterson, 118.
[16] Pippert, 130.

EIGHT
THE THIRD CONVERSATION: WHAT'S YOUR DREAM?

I'll never forget when I pulled the envelope out of the mailbox. I was only in 8th or 9th grade, so I didn't get a lot of mail, but this envelope had my name on it. Even better, it carried what appeared to be a promise that I would be rich. It read in big letters, "You have won $1,000,000!" I couldn't believe it! I won $1,000,000?! It was unbelievable!! Then I looked a little more closely at the envelope. In very small letters it read, "If you win, we'll say…" followed by the large print, "You have won $1,000,000!" So I hadn't already won $1,000,000, but I was in the running! That was all I needed to hear. To get a better chance at winning the money, I had to subscribe to a magazine or two. So I subscribed to *Car & Driver*, sent off my entry, and waited anxiously to find out when I would be rewarded my $1,000,000. Then I began to dream about what I would do with the money. Since I was just a short time away from getting a driver's license, I figured I would buy a Porsche 911 Turbo (it was on the cover of my first *Car & Driver* magazine). It was all-wheel-drive and could go from 0-60mph in 3.5 seconds—I still get butterflies just thinking about it.

I was so hopeful, and the power of that dream made my bad days better. Of course, I didn't win, unless they're still looking for me to tell me the good news! But I really thought I would, and the dream of winning brought hope and joy to my life. I learned two things from that experience that have stuck with me. First, if it looks too good to be true, it probably is. Second, and much more important, I learned how powerful a dream can be. My dream consumed my thoughts, made me feel happy, and empowered my imagination. Dreams aren't just goals and life ambitions; they drive us through life and lift our spirits. They make a bad day better, and they give us purpose. A dream is not just a dream—it is what builds our hope for the future, and hope is a powerful thing. When we talk about dreams, we're talking about hope.

An Italian man named Thomas Aquinas wrote about the essential characteristics of hope in his epic book *Summa Theologica*. Thomas was a Christian thinker in the 1200s, and his writing shaped the church and the way people thought about God. When he wrote about hope, he said that it had four qualities, or characteristics:[1]

1. Hope is good.
2. Hope is about the future.
3. Hope focuses on something challenging to accomplish.
4. Hope focuses on something that is possible.

A lot of people dream of winning the lottery, but that's more about luck. A dream that brings sustaining hope is one that evokes the kind of qualities Thomas Aquinas wrote about. It's not a daydream or a fantasy, but something that helps us envision what life could be like. A dream is a look into a future that brings good to our lives and the lives of those around us. It's something that can happen, but that will require more than luck to achieve.

We Need to Dream

Dreams contain our brightest hopes and reflect our inner

desires. My wife and I have a dream to one day own a sailboat that we can live on and sail all around the Caribbean. It makes me happy to think about it! I know that dream is probably at least 20 years away from being realized, but I still love to read about sailing and look at sailboats on the Internet. I especially like to dream about living on a sailboat after a tough day at work, or when things just aren't going well. That's because dreams bring light to the darkness. Hope is as important to life as light and air; it makes us excited, brings energy to our weakness, and helps us envision the future.[2] The opposite of hope is fear, which can stop us in our tracks and drive us to depression. But a dream is powerful! It can get us through times of depression and darkness in life by giving us hope for the future.[3]

The prophet Isaiah knew all about the power of hope, the power of a dream, the power of a vision for the future. He prophesied for 40-60 years in the latter half of the 8th Century BC at a dark time in Israel's history, and was an advisor to the Kings in Jerusalem. Isaiah and all of Judah had witnessed the destruction of the northern kingdom of Israel by Assyria, and Judah was forced under Assyrian rule for a time. Isaiah's job was to call the people of Judah to repentance and to give advice to the kings on behalf of God. He knew the times were dark, but he also had hope that came from God. Isaiah 40:30-31 talks about that hope, "Even youths shall faint and be weary, and young men shall fall exhausted; but they who wait for the LORD shall renew their strength; they shall mount up with wings like eagles; they shall run and not be weary; they shall walk and not faint" (ESV).

A dream is powerful! It can get us through times of depression and darkness in life by giving us hope for the future.

Four years ago I sat down with a shy teenager named Holly. She was a sophomore in high school and a committed Christian. Not only did she love the Lord, she made a commitment to share her faith in her high school as a missionary. This was not an easy commitment for a quiet and shy teenager to keep! But still, she did all she could and she dreamed about all that God could do. When we sat down together, she began to share one of her dreams with me; for her final project before graduation she wanted to bring an assembly program to her school to share the Gospel with all who attended. She was talking to me because I was in a position to help her with her dream.

At the time I was the director of a high school assembly program called "The Seven Project" that worked with schools to encourage students in their life journeys. We created customized school assemblies that focused on the needs of each school—drug avoidance, character development, academic achievement, dealing with bullies, etc. The program also worked with churches that would hold a second evening assembly to share the ultimate need in life—the need to know God and be reconciled to Him. The school assembly couldn't focus on God or faith at all, but Christian students in the school would mobilize for seven weeks before the assembly to invite their classmates and friends to come to the nighttime assembly, where the Gospel would be presented. Holly's dream was to bring this dual-assembly program to her school and to mobilize the Christian community to share the Gospel, and so she began to work towards that dream by meeting with me.

I explained how everything would need to work, as well as the major obstacles: the cost, getting permission from the school, and getting churches to support it. For most adults, this kind of process is overwhelming, but for a high school sophomore, it can seem impossible. She would need to raise nearly $6000, get at least three churches to work together to hold the night event, and convince her school that having this assembly would be a great idea. Holly was not fazed! She had a dream and she was determined to make it happen. Holly decided to submit her idea as the proposal for a required project that needed to be completed before graduation. She met with her principal, who expressed interest and agreed to travel with her to see the assembly in a nearby school that spring. In her junior year Holly got approval to proceed with her project, and then the hard work began.

The first challenge before her was to raise money to pay for the assemblies. She needed $500 to pay for the school assembly, and she needed $5500 to pay for the evening assembly. Her principal told her he would not set a date for the assembly until she figured out how to pay for it. She gave a presentation to her student council, who agreed to put the money forward for the school assembly. Then she started talking to churches. It didn't take long for several different churches to agree to work with her; the Church of God, the Assembly of God church, the Methodist Church, the Evangelical Free Church, and the Catholic Church all agreed to participate and to give money to make her dream a reality.

Then Holly really began to run into some real challenges. It seemed as though the school started to get nervous, and doubted the effectiveness of Holly's dream. Having raised all the money necessary, Holly kept trying to meet with the principal to set a date for the program, but she was continually frustrated as it kept getting pushed back. Time was running out for her to accomplish her project and get credit, and as time grew short, the chances of drawing all the churches together on short notice seemed slim. It would take at least two full months to mobilize the church community to get everything working properly, and we were starting to doubt it could happen. The principal finally set a date—it was only eight weeks away! The churches began to work towards the goal.

Then another setback occurred; instead of allowing the entire school to see the program, the principal decided to limit the program to freshman and sophomores. This was discouraging for Holly's dream because she was a senior and she wanted to impact her friends in her grade, but she didn't give up. Soon she was meeting with the principal again, and sharing her vision with a board member of the school district. In the last two weeks approaching the assembly, not only was it opened to the entire high school, but the middle school grades as well. Holly didn't give up on her dream, and now everything was building quickly to the launching point.

Then the day finally came! The assembly program came to her school, complete with lights, video, a professional skateboarder, and a former Harlem Globetrotter. Twelve hundred middle and high school students where challenged in the areas of integrity, character, drugs and alcohol avoidance, and to make positive choices. The principal was thrilled, and even expressed thankfulness that all grades were able to see the presentation. Holly, one of the quietest students I've ever met, stood before her entire school to introduce the assembly and to invite everyone to the evening event.

That night more than 400 people came and heard the Gospel! Many school board members were present and were pleased at the amount of community involvement in Holly's graduation project. The school had tried to have events in the past that gathered the community together like this, but nothing was ever accomplished on this scale. The attendance at the night event was ten times what their efforts had produced in the past! All of this happened because of a dream, a dream given by God to a quiet high school girl who was able to make a positive impact on her entire campus. She believed that something powerful was waiting; something that she could only see in her mind, and that God was leading her go after it. God gave her dream to her, and when it became a reality, her entire community was positively affected.

Dreams Give Life

When someone has a dream for the future that benefits humanity, or makes life better for others, it most likely comes from God and will point back to God. Hope also points to God, because it's the belief that something better exists, though we haven't yet seen it. It's the idea that a future that is better than the life we are experiencing now is waiting for us. The apostle Paul talks about the "blessed hope" in Titus 2:13, that Jesus would appear again on the earth in the future. Ultimately our hopes and dreams are rooted in the idea that something better is possible just over the horizon. Where do dreams come from? They can come from many places, but if they benefit others they probably come from God. Where does hope come from? Hope comes from God, and sustains us through life.

Just as Holly's dream gave life to her school, dreams can give us life today by providing hope for a better future and personal fulfillment. On the other hand, when we have no hope, when we're in a situation that causes us stress and anxiety, life can seem overwhelming and exhausting. Have you ever known anyone who was sick or injured badly? Did you know that hope can be a powerful aid in helping them recover? Scientific evidence has proven that people who have an attitude of hope are more likely to recover than people who do not believe they will get better.[4] Our dreams and our hope are life giving! When you connect to your friends' dreams, you connect to a central part of their being, and you help them focus on something that brings hope. Think about that—you could have conversations that inspire hope and vision for the future! The more you talk about someone's dream with them, the more they will associate you with hope and life.

> You could have conversations that inspire hope and vision for the future.

Discovering someone else's dream is one of my favorite conversations to have, and for most people, it's one of their favorite conversations to have too. When I meet someone new, if the conversation seems stalled or I'm not sure what to talk about, I just say, "So tell me about your dream. What would you do with your life if you could do anything?" It's not long before they open up and start sharing their inner hopes, aspirations, and even the path that life took to this point, leading them to their dream. Not long ago I made it a point to get to know a youth pastor that was fairly new to my network. I believed that God placed him on my heart, so I set an appointment for lunch to get to know him better. We sat down and had some small talk, but the conversation didn't gain much traction. Have you ever had a conversation like that? For some reason it's just hard to get someone talking, you get short answers to your questions that leave awkward pauses in the conversation. If you find yourself in that situation, it's a great moment to ask your friend about his dream. A dream can bring life to a lifeless conversation.

So, I asked him, "What's your dream? If you could do anything, what would it be?" The answer was instantaneous, and the conversation took off at a rapid pace. While he loved being a youth pastor, that's not what his ultimate dream was, and he had been waiting to talk with someone about it. He said, "That's so weird that you asked me that question. I've been thinking about it a lot, and was wondering who I could talk to." He wanted to plant a church one day, and he had been dreaming about how to do it. We didn't really know each other at the beginning of that lunch, but by the time we left the restaurant, we were friends who had had a good conversation. Not only that, but now he associates me with his dream, so he's usually happy to see me. Recently we got together again, and it didn't take long for him to begin talking about different kinds of churches, and the kind of church he wants to start. "I don't talk about this with anyone," he said, "You're the only person I can talk to about this." By talking to him about his dream, I was meeting a need in his life. What if you could meet some needs that no one else is meeting by talking to your friends about their dreams?

A God of Dreams

We serve a God of dreams; He gives the dreams, visions, hopes, and goals that move us toward our future. You don't have to turn too far in your Bible to realize that God works through dreams. We've been talking about the kind of dreams that give us direction in life. They are the vision for our future, our life goal, and our desire for what we want to be one day. In Scripture, God often spoke through the other kind of dream—the kind that occurs when we sleep. In fact, one of the reasons we use the word "dream" to talk about life goals and future vision is because God often gave people life goals and future vision in the Bible through sleeping dreams. God told Abraham that he would give his descendants the land that became Israel in a dream. God appeared to King Solomon in a dream in 1 Kings 3, and told Solomon he would be the wisest man in the history of the world. God spoke to Jesus' father in a dream and told him to take Mary and Jesus to Egypt. But the most well-known dreamer in Scripture is Joseph, whose story is told in Genesis 37-40.

Joseph was one of the youngest of Jacob's 12 sons and, along with his brothers, he is one of the founders of the 12 tribes of Israel. Although Jacob had many sons, he loved Joseph more than all the rest, giving him a special coat. Unfortunately, like many families today, Joseph's family was dysfunctional, and his brothers hated him. In fact, the Bible states that their hatred was so great they couldn't even say a kind word to him. It didn't really help matters when God started to give Joseph dreams about the future. Joseph had two dreams in Genesis 37, and both were about his family and their future. In the first dream, Joseph saw 12 bundles of grain, one for him and each of his brothers. All of the bundles of grain came and bowed down to Joseph's. When Joseph told his brothers the dream, they were outraged. They could not believe Joseph expected that he would one day rule over them.

In the second dream, Joseph saw the sun and the moon and 11 stars, and they were all bowing down to him. This time, he told his dream to his father as well as his brothers. His father wasn't happy about the dream, and scolded Joseph for dreaming that his family would bow down to him. Have you ever had one of your dreams shot down by someone you looked up to? It's one of the most disheartening things that can happen, and can discourage you from dreaming again. But Joseph held onto his dream, and even though his father had corrected him, his father also kept the dream in his mind. Joseph's brothers, on the other hand, wanted to forget the dream, and they wanted to forget Joseph. In one of the most horrifying stories in Scripture, Joseph's brothers threw him into a pit, and then sold him into slavery. They took his robe, covered it with animal blood, and told their father that a wild animal had killed Joseph. Jacob thought his son was dead, and Joseph's brothers thought they were rid of him for good.

> We serve a God of dreams; He gives the dreams, visions, hopes, and goals that move us toward our future.

So Joseph was sold like a piece of property to traders who would carry him off and sell him to the highest bidder. He had dreamed of being the head of his family, but instead he would probably never see his family again. The traders took Joseph to Egypt, where he was sold to an Egyptian official named Potiphar to work in his home. It did not take long for Joseph to rise to the top of Potiphar's household, and he was placed in charge of everything in the home, including the other servants. Things were finally looking up for Joseph, but unfortunately, it didn't last long. Joseph found favor in Potiphar's eyes, but Potiphar's wife was sexually attracted to Joseph, and soon acted on it. One day, when Joseph was the only servant in house, Potiphar's wife tried to seduce him. Joseph ran away, but not before Potiphar's wife ripped his coat off of him. Embarrassed and angered by Joseph's rejection, she accused him of trying to seduce her, and Potiphar had Joseph thrown in jail.

Now Joseph had gone from favored son to slave, from slave to head of the household, from head of the household to being an inmate in an ancient Egyptian prison. This did not look anything like the dream God had given him. But God was still at work in Joseph's life, orchestrating times and events to make the dream become a reality. While a prisoner, Joseph found favor with the head jailer, and was soon put in charge of all the prisoners. Always a man of dreams, Joseph got the chance to interpret the dreams of two of Pharaoh's employees, whom Pharaoh had thrown into jail. Two years later, when one of the employees was back working in Pharaoh's service, Pharaoh had a dream that he could not understand. Soon the employee remembered Joseph, and told Pharaoh all about him. Joseph was pulled out of jail and interpreted Pharaoh's dream so impressively that Pharaoh decided give Joseph a job. The dream God had given Pharaoh predicted a seven-year surplus of food, followed by a seven-year famine. Pharaoh saw God at work in Joseph during the interpretation, and decided that Joseph was the man to manage Egypt's food supply. And so Pharaoh placed Joseph in charge of the entire nation of Egypt. Through all of this, Joseph never forgot the dream God had given him.

The famine came after seven years of surplus, and it didn't just affect Egypt; it affected the entire Middle East. Joseph's father and brothers soon began to run out of food, and it was rumored Egypt was the only place with food to spare. So Joseph's father sent his sons to Egypt to try to get some food for the family, and when they arrived, they had to bow down to Joseph. His dream had become a reality! After a tear-filled reunion, Joseph arranged for his entire family to come and live in the safety and surplus of Egypt. He forgave his brothers of their evil actions against him, and provided for them and their families until his death.

When he was just a boy, God gave Joseph a dream that took decades to become a reality, and Joseph had many struggles and setbacks along the way. But the dream was always there! Think about what God gave to Joseph when He gave him a dream:

- **Hope in a difficult family situation.** Joseph did not have a good family situation. His brothers despised him, but God gave Joseph hope through his dream that one day things would change.

- **Vision for leadership.** God gave Joseph the vision of leadership. Joseph was able to see himself, not as a younger child, but as a leader over others. Wherever Joseph went, he conducted himself as a leader, and God put him in positions of leadership.
- **A sustaining help during dark times.** Joseph was a slave, an accused rapist, and a prisoner, but no one could take his dream away from him. Dreams bring hope, and they help us get through life's difficulties.
- **Skills for the future.** Because God gave Joseph a dream, Joseph understood that dreams were from God and could be interpreted for life's situations. The skill of interpreting dreams got Joseph out of prison, and earned him a position of authority in the land of Egypt.

God gave Joseph a dream, and Joseph's dream defined who he would become and how he would get there. Can God speak to your friends through their dreams for the future? Yes! Is it possible for God to use you to help your friends interpret their dreams and find God in the process? Of course! The key to unlocking the power of a dream is having a great conversation.

> Joseph's dream defined who he would become and how he would get there.

Having the Conversation

Every good conversation begins and flows with good questions. Here are some questions to get you going, but you can always develop your own and allow the conversation to flow naturally:

- ***If you could do anything with your life, and there were no limitations, what would you do?*** This is a great way to start a conversation about a dream. When limitations such as time and money are eliminated, people are free to express what they really dream about doing. Another way of asking this question is saying, *"If you knew that you couldn't fail, what would you do?"*

- ***What's stopping you from doing that?*** This is a good follow-up question to the one above. It can help your friends start to carve out a roadmap for accomplishing their dreams.
- ***What's your dream in life?*** The direct approach is sometimes best. This is especially true if someone already knows what he wants to do. That will not always be the case, but sometimes people have already given it a lot of thought.
- ***What needs to happen for your dream to come true?*** This is a follow-up question to the one directly above. You can help your friends begin to process their dreams (the next steps, obstacles, etc.) by asking this question.
- ***What are you best at? In what ways could you use that to try to accomplish your dream?*** With this question you can help your friends understand that their current skills can be useful in accomplishing their dreams. There's an old saying, "God wastes nothing." If someone has a skill they are particularly good at, it's likely going to be useful in achieving their hopes and desires.
- ***What's the biggest or most important thing you need to do to take a step towards accomplishing your dream?*** This kind of question can really help show your friends that you care about their dreams. It can also help your friends move forward with accomplishing what they really want in life.

At some point, you will try to talk to a friend about his dream and he won't know what it is. Maybe he's never thought about it before. In that case, here's a great series of questions to ask to get him thinking about his dreams:

- ***Do you think we all have a purpose? What would yours be?*** Not everyone will be prepared to answer this question. A lot people have never thought about it before, but this can really get someone thinking. The answer may not directly be his life's dream, but it's a way of moving towards it.

- ***If you could fix one problem in the world, what would it be? What is it about that situation that compels you?*** This is a great question to get people dreaming. Follow up with, *"What would be the best way to fix this problem? What would you do to get started?"*
- ***In your ideal world, what would life be like for you in 10 years?*** Help your friend get a vision for himself a decade down the road. This is a ten-year dream. Follow-up with, *"What steps can you take to make sure this vision becomes reality?"*
- ***What did you want to be "when you grew up"? When you were a little kid?*** Often, our desires as children are strong indicators of what is in our hearts and what we truly love to do. Some follow-up questions: *What made you want to be that? Do you still dream about it? What needs to happen for you to become what you wanted to be?*
- ***What's the most fulfilling thing you've done in life? What was significant about it?*** By exploring your friend's life experience and what he's found to be the most satisfying in life, you can help him discover his dream. Follow-up with, *"Would you consider doing that for a living? What would you need to do to make that a lifestyle or occupation?"*
- ***What do you most want to be or do before you die?*** This is a "bucket list" type of question, and there may be a lot of answers. But the answers are a window into a lot of "mini-dreams" that lay in the hearts of many of your friends. If one of their answers makes them excited, go deeper. Simply say, *"Tell me more about that."*

It's important that you always encourage your friends in their dreams. They may say something that surprises you, or that you consider to be impossible. They may even say something that makes you want to laugh, but it's not your place to tell them it can't happen. If you discourage someone in his dream, you do the same thing that Joseph's brothers did when they mocked his dream. Maybe God himself planted the dream; only the individual can ultimately know if that's the case.

Believe in your friends! It's important that you believe their dreams can become a reality. It takes discipline and maturity to listen to someone's dream, and it takes love and compassion to ask powerful questions about that dream. It requires faith for you to dream with them, affirming that it's possible for the dream to come true. Our friends need to be encouraged and affirmed in their dreams, especially if they are dreaming of doing something different or unusual.[5] When God gives someone a dream or a vision, it's often one that affects change, maybe even changes history. The dreams God gives always require large amounts of faith and vision to see as reality. By having great conversations and affirming your friends' dreams, you can help them discover the God who gives dreams.

Connecting to the Gospel

Dreaming a big dream requires big faith, and since we come to God in faith, a dream is a natural way to connect to God. Though we cannot see the result of our dreams presently, we move through life with the certainty that one day we will see our dreams come true. Dreaming drives us to a life of hope, because we understand that life can improve and that something more meaningful and enriching is around the corner.[6] To dream is to exercise faith, because faith is being sure of what we hope for and certain of what we do not see (Hebrews 11:1). If you want to connect people to God through a dream conversation, then you must first be a person who dreams, a person of hope! One of the most well-known atheists who ever lived was a Marxist named Earnest Bloch. Bloch argued that Christianity's greatest contribution to the world

> Dreaming a big dream requires big faith, and since we come to God in faith, a dream is a natural way to connect to God.

was the introduction of the "principle of hope."[7] In fact, he believed that you couldn't truly think as a Christian unless you viewed the future as it *could* be. So, what *is* your dream? What can God do through you? What are you hoping for? If you've never thought about your dream before, go back to the questions listed above (the questions meant for you to ask your friend), and ask them of yourself. Write down your answers. Identify your own dream.

As your friendships progress and you begin to ask about your friends' dreams, it will only be natural for them to ask you about your dream. When that time comes, I hope you can share a dream that God has given you. Because when you get the opportunity to share your dream, you also get to share the motivation behind your dream. If God is motivating you to find a cure for world hunger, talk about the God behind your dream. If God has given you a dream, let Him shine through it. Sammy Ray Skaggs wrote about discovering a "God-dream," and what a God-dream looks like. One way to know if your dream is from God is to use the list of characteristics he came up with:[8]

- A God-dream will never contradict scriptural wisdom.
- A God-dream will bring peace to your life, even if it conflicts with worldly wisdom.
- A God-dream can stand the test of discernment and even persecution.
- A God-dream will always be "others focused," not the other way around.
- A God-dream will take time to be realized.
- A God-dream needs the power of God to pull it off.
- A God-dream needs wisdom from God to navigate through the pitfalls and challenges created by it.

- A God-dream will draw fire from the enemy and anyone he chooses to use to hinder and suppress it from being realized.
- A God-dream will have both valley and mountaintop seasons

Make a commitment to be a dreamer, to discover a dream from God for your life, and to share that dream with others.

Did you know that God has a dream? He has a vision and a desire that drives so much of what He does. God's dream is that all of humanity would be saved and brought into fellowship with Himself. That is why he is so patient with us, because he doesn't want anyone to perish, but wants everyone to come to repentance (2 Peter 3:9). He wants all people to be saved, and to come to a knowledge of the truth (1 Timothy 2:4). God is drawing individuals to Jesus, even as you read this (John 6:44). That is why he sent the Holy Spirit into the world, so that the world could be convicted concerning sin, and righteousness, and judgment. He also sent the Holy Spirit to empower us to be His witnesses. Imagine—God can use your friends' dreams, and your dream, to accomplish His dream. Discover your dream, ask others about their dreams, and point them to the One who gives dreams.

> God can use your friends' dreams, and your dream, to accomplish His dream.

Praying

It was in a dream that Solomon asked God for wisdom, and God granted Solomon's request. You could exercise some wisdom of your own by praying for God to grant you a dream. Jesus said, "Ask and it will be given to you; seek, and you will find; knock, and it will be opened to you" (Luke 11:19). Ask God to give you a dream, and also ask him for the courage to ask others about their dreams. Pray for God to give you discernment, and to speak to you through the Holy Spirit so that you will be able to know the best time to ask somebody about his dream. Pray for God to give you faith to see the future, discipline and maturity to listen to the dreams of others, and love and compassion to ask powerful questions and affirm their dreams.

---

[1] Thomas Aquinas, *Summa Theologica*, Benzinger Bros./Accordance electronic ed. (Altamonte Springs: OakTree Software, 2004), I-II.40.1.
[2] Glenn Tinder, *The Fabric of Hope: An Essay* (Atlanta: Scholars Press, 1999), 13.
[3] Patrick Shade, *Habits of Hope: A Pragmatic Theory* (Nashville: Vanderbilt University Press, 2001), 6.
[4] Shade, 6.
[5] Joel Comiskey et al, 41.
[6] Edward Wojcicki, *A Crisis of Hope in the Modern World* (Chicago: The Thomas More Press, 1991), 151.
[7] James L. Muyskens, *The Sufficiency of Hope: The Conceptual Foundations of Relgion* (Philadelphia: Temple University Press, 1979), 93).
[8] Comiskey et al, 42.

NINE
THE FOURTH CONVERSATION:
WHERE DO DREAMS COME FROM? DOES GOD EXIST?

Zombies are so hot right now. There have been 15 major movies featuring zombies released in theaters since 2000. Survival companies have popped up across the nation, selling kits and emergency supplies to help us get ready for the so-called "zombie apocalypse." You can even sign up to run in a zombie-themed race, where you only cross the finish line if you can avoid getting taken out by the undead! I'll even admit that on any given day you're likely to find me playing "Plants vs. Zombies" on my iPhone. But the crowning jewel in the zombie empire is the TV show, "The Walking Dead." This show is so popular that nearly 20 million people tune in to watch each episode! It's the most popular show on cable television, and even outranks football in viewers by almost 25%! You don't have to look too far today to know that we, as a society, are enthralled with the afterlife.

We are fascinated with life after death. What happens when we die? That's a question that nearly every person asks at some point in life. We are fascinated with the future. Hopes and dreams deal with the future. Zombies deal with the future (though if that's a dream, it's a nightmare!). The final horizon for all people is death, and hope in death rests in the ideal that life (better life) exists beyond the horizon of death. Simply put, our hopes and our dreams point to life beyond death, and life beyond death points to God.

I've often wondered how an atheist thinks about life after death. Interestingly, zombies may be the limit of an atheist's hope for an afterlife. Most religions in the world have an answer for the question, "What happens when we die?" But atheism leaves very little hope and optimism when it comes to death. In an article for *Esquire* magazine, atheist Stephen Marche wrote, "Atheism does not provide a very comforting way to deal with the dead. Christians and others have prayer and visions of an afterlife. Pagans have ghosts and spirit ancestors with whom one can negotiate. Atheists like myself have rotting corpses and oblivion. And zombie movies."[1] Wow, that's pretty hopeless! Atheism ultimately points to very little hope, but belief in God's existence opens up avenues of vision, dreams, possibilities, and hope for ultimate good and an ultimate "Do-Gooder."

When I try to begin a conversation about God, it's not unusual for the person I'm talking with to say, "I'm an atheist."

However, very few people in the world are actually atheists. Most people say this to avoid having an uncomfortable conversation about a topic that could change their life. This is especially true if I don't know them because it can be uncomfortable to talk with someone about something so personal as faith when you're not already friends. This is a conversation that dives directly into the question of God's existence, but you shouldn't be afraid to talk with your friends about God, especially if you've already had the three previous conversations in this book. If you've gotten to know them by asking about their story, then it's likely they know something about your story. If you've taken an interest in what they do, then it's likely they know you're interested in God. If you've asked about their dreams, then it's natural for you to encourage them in their dreams by pointing them to God. By the time you're ready to have the fourth conversation, you've earned the right to be heard on this topic.

Very few people in the world are actually atheists. Most people say this to avoid having an uncomfortable conversation about a topic that could change their life.

Everybody Worships

Almost everyone worships something. Most people have some kind of god they bow to in life. Very few people claiming to be atheists today are actual atheists. The American intellectualist and author David Foster Wallace said, "In the day-to-day trenches of adult life, there is actually no such thing as atheism. There is no such thing as not worshipping. Everybody worships. The only choice we get is *what* to worship. And an outstanding reason for choosing some sort of God or spiritual-type thing to worship—be it Jesus Christ or Allah, be it Yahweh or the Wiccan mother-goddess or the Four

Noble Truths or some intangible set of ethical principles—is that pretty much anything else you worship will eat you alive."[2] He went on to give several examples of this; if you worship beauty you'll never be beautiful enough, if you worship money you'll never be rich enough, if you worship intellect you'll probably feel stupid most of the time, if you worship power you'll likely feel weak and powerless. Almost everyone worships something.

That's why Classical Atheism (the belief that God doesn't exist) has given way to something called "New Atheism." New Atheism has become very popular today because it refuses to argue that God doesn't exist; it has given up that argument as too difficult to prove and impossible to win. So instead of arguing against God's existence, New Atheism argues that religion is evil, and that the *concept* of God has done more harm to this world than good. If you've ever encountered a real atheist today, you know exactly what I'm talking about. They can't prove that God doesn't exist, but they can prove that some religious people have caused pain and suffering in the world, so the conclusion is that God can't be real or shouldn't be worshipped. In the view of New Atheism, religion is the cause of great evil, and the power for good comes from within humanity and exists to make humanity better. There may be an all-powerful force that drives the creation and the expansion of the universe, but it's not a traditional god—and certainly not the Christian God. New Atheists tout the saying, "You can be good without God."

New Atheists are correct when they say that religion, and even the church, have done some wrong to society. From the Crusades to modern day sex scandals, there can be no doubt that religious people are just as capable of evil as non-religious people. However, the New Atheists argument is ultimately extremely faulty, because atheist leaders did far more evil and damage to society, just in the last hundred years, than religious leaders ever have. A simple look back on the 1900s proves this to be true. Two atheist leaders came to power around World

War II, Joseph Stalin in Russia and Mao Zedong (also known as Mao Tse-tung) in China. Stalin is believed to have killed 34-49 million Russians who opposed him in some way from 1928-1954.[3] Mao killed 45 million Chinese in just four years, from 1958-1962.[4] When God doesn't exist, morality disappears, and even mass murder can be accepted by a society. That's one reason why educated atheists today do not argue against God's existence, but for the evil of religion instead; they know classical atheism has led to far more evil than any religion has. Atheism fails the moral test. In the end, the world needs God and the New Atheists know it, but they don't believe the world needs organized religion.

Is it possible to be good apart from God? The answer is yes, and you probably know some atheists who are good people. But morals inevitably point to a higher good. C.S. Lewis, in *The Case for Christianity*, notes that when two people are arguing the determining factor between them will be who is right and who is wrong.[5] In spite of their differences, one of them must be right and one of them must be wrong. The concepts of right and wrong are universal to humanity, and in spite of the differences among various cultures there is a universal recognition that certain values pertain to all mankind. So where does the idea of right and wrong come from? Where does the concept of good and evil come from? If someone maintains that God does not exist, then the idea of the "highest good" has been abandoned. And without a "highest good" morality doesn't have a firm foundation, and it can destabilize into the kind of anarchy seen in the leadership of Stalin and Mao. It's not that morality apart from God is impossible, it's that it naturally produces moral instability.[6]

A second failure of atheism is that science fails to answer all questions as it relates to the earth and the universe. The Big Bang theory, for example, can explain how the universe came to exist in its current state, but it cannot explain the cause or the origin of the energy behind the "bang." In fact, science also states that energy cannot be created or destroyed, meaning that whatever energy caused the universe to come into existence was itself in existence before the creation event. A third failure is that atheism fails to address the deep questions of human existence such as, "Why do I exist? What is my purpose?" and "Where does hope come from?"

We've seen some good reasons why atheism if faulty, and you may be tempted to use this chapter to win an argument against an atheist, but that's not why I've written it. In fact, I hope you'll avoid getting into an argument and use the points in this chapter to raise curiosity about God instead. When you get into an argument, you create an adversary of the person you want to reach. That's bad news for a friendship, and it's bad news for the Gospel. If you've created an adversary, you've given someone a reason not to like you. But if you can have a rational discussion, you can quickly make a friend who will enjoy having a good conversation with you. The truth is most New Atheists have suffered some sort of loss, or been hurt by some form of religion or by an individual Christian, and that's why they're so opposed to the church and to God. What they really need is a friend who will hear out those concerns. The point of the conversation is not to argue, nor is it to prove yourself right, the point is to help people reach the conclusion that God exists. Just give the clues that will lead to God's existence, and let the Holy Spirit do the rest of the work.

> When you get into an argument, you create an adversary of the person you want to reach.

Having the Conversation

Every good conversation begins and flows with good questions. Here are some questions to get you going, but you can always develop your own and allow the conversation to flow naturally:

- ***Where does hope come from?*** Hope comes from the idea that something good or better is just over the horizon. What could be better on the horizon than a God who loves us and wants us to join Him in heaven? This is a great indirect way of broaching the subject of God.
- ***Where do dreams come from?*** This is good if you had a conversation about your friend's dream. Otherwise you may not want to use it. Especially ask this question if their dream leads to the benefit of people. This is another great indirect way to ask about their belief in God.
- ***Have you ever wondered if God is real?*** It's okay to start here, especially if you've got a good friendship and you've been active in the other conversations. They may say no, or they may say something that offends you, but that's okay. Just listen! Get them talking about God. Follow up with, *"Why do you feel that way?"*
- ***Do you think much about spiritual things?*** This can open the door to a lot of good conversations. The "spiritual" world is broad, so also remember that you may be opening up a can of worms. They may talk about ghosts, or card readers, or angels and demons. That's okay, just get them talking about spirituality. Even a conversation about ghosts points to the existence of the supernatural, and God himself is supernatural. When the opportunity comes in the conversation, just say, *"What about God? Do you think there is a God?"*
- ***Do you think God is good? Why or why not?*** Again, you don't have to agree with them. They may have some very dark ideas about God, but that doesn't matter. What's important is to have the conversation.
- ***How is it possible for the universe to work together so well?*** This is a great conversation that's been had all through history by philosophers and theologians. We'll talk a little about having this conversation below, but in short, the clockwork nature of creation points to a "clockmaker."

- ***What made it possible for me to know right and wrong when I was a kid, before anyone taught me?*** This is another great conversation that philosophers have had for millennia. You can read more about it in the rest of this chapter, and we've already talked about it a little bit. Get them thinking about the nature of morality. *Where does morality come from?*
- ***What causes nearly all humanity to have a universal sense of right and wrong?*** This philosophical question points to a great power in the universe that connects to all mankind—it's God! This is a deep question that may provoke some different answers, but don't be afraid to point to God.

The Apostle Paul's Case for God

In Romans 1-2, the Apostle Paul makes a case for Gentiles (non-Jews) having the ability to know about God, even though they didn't receive the revelations the Jews did in the Old Testament. Essentially, he was arguing that it's possible to know about God even if you've never been told about God or read about Him in the Bible. He made his case by appealing to two different pieces of logic. In Romans 1:19-20 he wrote, "For what can be known about God is plain to them, because God has shown it to them. For his invisible attributes, namely, his eternal power and divine nature, have been clearly perceived, ever since the creation of the world, in the things that have been made. So they are without excuse" (ESV). His first piece of logic was nature; the earth, the universe, and the human being. Paul believed that the clockwork nature of the universe couldn't have happened by accident; God must have designed it.

The second point Paul makes is in Romans 2:14-15a, "For when Gentiles, who do not have the law, by nature do what the law requires, they are a law to themselves, even though they do not have the law. They show that the work of the law is written on their hearts, while their conscience also bears witness..."

(ESV). His second piece of logic was the human conscience; the idea that almost all humans know what right and wrong are and feel badly when they do not do the right thing. Paul was saying that men know what right and wrong are naturally, and that doesn't happen by accident; a Creator imprints it upon their minds. These two points, nature and conscience, are the two key questions to engage in when trying to discuss God's existence: What makes the universe work so well? What causes the sense of right and wrong in us?

Two points—nature and conscience—are the two key questions to engage in when trying to discuss God's existence.

When most Christians are asked how they know God exists, they're likely to say, "Because the Bible says so." But if someone doesn't believe in the Bible or the Church, they won't listen to what's being said. The Apostle Paul, on the other hand, didn't make the case for God's existence from his Bible (the Old Testament). Instead, he made his case from naturally occurring sources from outside the Bible. Those sources were also used by the popular philosophies of his day to make the same case—that God (or a god) exists and has created the universe and man. Paul was using a philosophy called "Stoicism." The fact that he used a philosophy found outside of the Bible tells us two things: first, Paul approved of the logic of the Stoicism,[7] and second, Paul could discuss God's existence without using Scripture. This is important, because if someone is going to come to Jesus, they must first believe in God, and if they don't believe in God, you probably won't convince them using God's book. Paul was a good Jew and could have argued from the Old Testament all day long if he wanted to, but he chose not to! He arrived at the same conclusion of the Hebrew Scriptures using secular arguments. This is important for establishing a conversation with non-believers; you do not need to start with God (or scripture) to arrive at the existence of God. The discussion should begin in an experience and knowledge of the universe that is common to everyone, in this case it's the experience of nature and of morality.

God is Seen in Nature

In the 1934, an eight-year-old boy looked up into the night sky and began to dream. What was out there? What lay beyond the stars? What caused the universe to work like it does and what keeps it going? Nature, and everything in it, had an enchantment for him—it was special and attractive. This fascination led him to a sense of destiny. He felt like he had a purpose in life. The boys name was Allan, and he said, "The world was magic, there was something and not nothing."[8] He was amazed and surprised by the cosmos and by the earth. His sense of destiny led him to become an astronomer so he could learn all about how the universe worked. On his way to becoming a great astronomer, Allan became convinced that only science was real. The mystery of the universe he loved as child was replaced by the cold hard facts of science.

Allan's job as an astronomer was to examine and confirm, or disprove, Edwin Hubble's theory of universal expansion. That means he was trying to prove, by measuring the distance and age of stars, that the universe was expanding in the same way everywhere from a central starting point. In other words, his job was to prove the Big Bang Theory. As he worked towards proving this scientific principle, he also came to another, more mysterious conclusion: the universe cannot have so neatly and precisely expanded without some being, or power, to organize it. He soon came to the realization that God must exist. The more he looked into the universe, the more it became "less and less clear that all this could have occurred without an ordering principle; and that ordering principle I guess I called God in order to give a name to the mystery."[9] In other words, not only did Allan confirm the Big Bang Theory, but he also came to the conclusion that God must have caused it. Allan Sandage was one of the most respected astronomers in history. He discovered the first quasar, was the first man to scientifically determine an age for the universe, and he won the Crafoord Prize, the Royal Swedish Academy's version of the Nobel for his work. His study of nature and the universe, and his inability to solve all the mysteries his studies uncovered, led him to the conclusion that God exists.

John Calvin, a great Christian thinker and preacher who lived in the 1500s said nature is the "theater of the glory of God."[10] Psalm 19 reads, "The heavens are telling the glory of God; and the firmament proclaims his handiwork" (NRSV). But it's not just Christians who point to nature to explain God's existence. Aristotle's teachings did the same thing! Aristotle believed God was real and could be seen through the actions of nature, that a "single agent" spurred all matter in the universe to action, and that "single agent" was God.[11] Another philosopher who lived at the same time as Paul, Epictetus, argued that when something is built (buildings or monuments) we know that someone built it; it didn't happen by chance. Then he argued that the earth was the same way—it's a visible and created object that must have a designer and a creator.[12]

Science leaves too many questions unanswered, nature reveals too much mystery, and the universe works together too perfectly for there not to be a Creator. You don't need to draw this conclusion for your friend, and it may be better if you let them figure it out by asking questions, rather than giving answers. Just raise various questions and curiosities, and let your friend think about them. Anyone who seeks the truth must come to the conclusion that there are too many mysteries that cannot be answered by scientific discovery and reasoning. But those mysteries can be solved by God's existence! If life didn't happen by chance, only two options remain—necessity and design.[13] The argument for necessity has too many gaps that cannot be explained scientifically, which leaves the broad possibility for a designer. Let your friend reach this conclusion, because in the end it's more reasonable to believe in God than not too. It's easier to believe in a designer than to believe in chance.

This designer, the One who caused the universe to come into existence, is the one Thomas Aquinas refers to as "the highest cause of the whole universe."[14] Just like the astronomer Allan Sandage, I used to love to go out as a child and gaze at the stars. I loved doing it as a kid, I loved doing it as a teenager, and I love doing it today. I even asked my parents for a telescope one year for Christmas. When I look up at the cosmos, there is a divine sense that God is out there. There is a feeling that He is powerful, that He is connected to us, and that He is calling to us! A lot of people feel this same calling, but are afraid to express it because science is perceived to disprove God's existence. Great scientists like Allan Sandage teach us differently, and you can draw these feelings out of your friends by talking about the universe and its unexplained mysteries.

God is Seen in Morality

About 100 years ago a man named G.K. Chesterton was on the road to becoming a strong Christian, but he didn't know it yet. Chesterton had some exposure to Christianity as a boy, but had become an agnostic by the age of 16. An agnostic is someone who believes that an ultimate force exists in the universe (God), but that this force is unknowable and hasn't yet been identified by any religion. Most people who call themselves atheists today are actually agnostics. Chesterton had a brilliant mind. He wrote a weekly column for the *Illustrated London News* and wrote the novels *The Man Who Was Thursday* and *The Napoleon of Notting Hill.* He started to form his own religious philosophy based on his logical observations of human behavior and the natural world.[15] After observing the way the world works, he developed a system of thinking about life and God that he thought was all his own. He was surprised to learn that his private philosophy was nearly identical to the beliefs of Christianity. He joined the church in 1922 and became one of its greatest defenders and writers during his time. He came to Christ based upon his observations of the outer world (the universe) and the inner world (human nature).

Just as the experience of nature is universal to everyone, so is the understanding of morality. There is a universal sense of what is right and what is wrong. This is what the Apostle Paul meant when he wrote, "the work of the law is written on their hearts, while their conscience also bears witness" (Romans 2:15 ESV2). Paul was making the case that a divine morality is common to all humanity. This would be present in the Jew, the Christian, and the pagan, and even in those who did not believe. The Hebrew tradition called this undeniable sense of morality the "heart," and the Greeks and Romans called it the "conscience,"[16] the understanding of right and wrong.[17] And this sense of right and wrong, this conscience, this heart, is present in all mankind.

Now it's true that some values, laws, and morals will differ from one culture to another. However, there is a global understanding that right and wrong exist, and certain universal behaviors apply to all cultures. Among them are respect for life and the value and protection of offspring. So there is moral truth that is true for every culture on earth. Where does that come from? How does that happen? C.S. Lewis thought about it like this:

> "These, then, are the two points I wanted to make. First, that human beings, all over the earth, have this curious idea that they ought to behave in a certain way, and cannot really get rid of it. Secondly, that they do not in fact behave in that way. They know the law of nature; they break it. These two facts are the foundation of all clear thinking about ourselves in the universe we live in."[18]

Lewis began his journey as a Christian, but became an atheist after experiencing the horror of World War I. In spite of his mental wounds, he came back to the idea that God must exist when he considered the concept of "right" and "wrong." He wrote, "My argument against God was that the universe seems so cruel and unjust. But how had I got this idea of just and unjust? A man does not call a line crooked unless he has some idea of a straight line."[19]

Could this universal sense of right and wrong occur in every culture on earth, in every person, by accident? When I was a child no one taught me how to lie, I knew how to do it automatically. Maybe I broke something, or maybe I stole something, but when I was asked about it I lied because I didn't want to get into trouble. I was too young, too little, to understand right and wrong logically, but I still knew something was wrong, so I lied. I also knew, instinctively, that lying was wrong. How could I have known all of this, not in my mind, but in my heart, my conscience, if no one had ever taught me? It was because right and wrong had been imprinted on my heart before I could even logically understand what they were. And this conscience is universal to all mankind. The best explanation for this universal conscience is God's existence—God exists, he is moral, and we bear his imprint in our universal understanding of morality. When writing about this moral curiosity and logical impossibility, Stephen Evans and Zachary Manis came to the following three-step conclusion: (1) Unless there is a God, there cannot be universal moral rights and wrongs, (2) but there are universal rights and wrongs, (3) therefore, there is a God.[20]

Not only does our instinctive morality point to the existence of God, but it points to the God of the Bible. In a sense, all religions are an attempt to respond to our understanding (through nature and morality) of God's existence, but most religions get it wrong. John Calvin wrote about a "seed of religion," as well as an idea of God "inscribed on the hearts of all."[21] He backs up this thought by pointing out "from the beginning of the world there has been no region, no city, in short, no household, that could do without religion."[22] But the truly great movements of morality and justice have come from Christianity, and from its predecessor, Judaism. Reinhold Niebuhr said, "Every genuine passion for social justice will always contain the religious element within it."[23] But only in Christianity will you find the equality of people expressed like this, "There is neither Jew nor Gentile, neither slave nor free, nor is there male and female, for you are all one in Christ Jesus" (Galatians 3:28 NIV), or "Here there is no Jew or a Gentile, circumcised or uncircumcised, barbaric, uncivilized, slave or free. Christ is all that matters, and He lives in all of us" (Colossians 3:11 NLT). Only in Christianity will you find equality in marriage stated like this, "Submit to one another out of reverence for Christ" (Ephesians 5:21 NIV).

The Real Question

I've given you some great thoughts and conversation starters to get your friends talking, but the real question that may convince your friend to believe in God is this—why do *you* believe in God? Can you talk about it? Can you share the story of why belief in God matters to you? A well-known researcher and medical doctor named Francis Collins was confronted with this kind of story one day in his medical practice. Collins, who led the Human Genome Project and served as Director of the National Institutes of Health, told the story in his 2007 book *The Language of God.*[24] Showing a lot of promise as a medical student, Collins decided it would be "convenient" to be an atheist, meaning he wouldn't have to deal with the question of God. Then one day in his medical practice a patient began sharing her faith with him. Then she asked, "What about you? What do you believe?" As knowledgeable as he was about the human body and science, he struggled to come up with an answer, finally stating that he didn't believe anything. He later wrote, "It suddenly seemed like a very thin answer. And that was unsettling."

After that, Collins went on a long search for God's existence. He read some of C.S. Lewis' writings and questioned a pastor extensively. He finally found Jesus in one of the ways the Apostle Paul reasoned about. He wrote his experience in his book:

> I had to make a choice. A full year had passed since I decided to believe in some sort of God, and now I was being called to account. On a beautiful fall day, as I was hiking in the Cascade Mountains during my first trip west of the Mississippi, the majesty and beauty of God's creation overwhelmed my resistance. As I rounded a corner and saw a beautiful and unexpected frozen waterfall, hundreds of feet high, I knew the search was over. The next morning, I knelt in the dewy grass as the sun rose and surrendered to Jesus Christ.[25]

Francis Collins has a powerful story to tell about how he came to believe in God's existence. But he only has that story to tell because one of his patients shared her story of belief in God, which caused him to think about his own belief. So what's your story? Why do you believe in God?

Prayer

If you've been keeping up with the conversations in this book, then you likely know how to pray for your friends already. Now begin to pray that God would give you a specific opportunity to talk with them about His existence. Pray for God to help you understand and craft your own powerful story of why you believe. Pray for moments with your friend in God's creation that will help you to open up a conversation. Pray for the chance to observe some great moral action in progress, so that you can make a connection to God. Pray that the Holy Spirit helps you discern the right time and place to open up this philosophical conversation.

---

[1] Stephen Marche, "Why Zombies are Everywhere Now," *Esquire.com*, June 19, 2013, under "The Culture Blog," http://www.esquire.com/blogs/culture/why-zombies-are-everywhere (accessed April 21, 2014).

[2] David Foster Wallace, "David Foster Wallace on Life and Work," *Wall Street Journal* online, September 19, 2008 under "Books," http://online.wsj.com/news/articles/SB1221782119664560 7 (accessed April 21, 2014).

[3] Iosif G. Dyadkin, *Unnatural Deaths in the USSR, 1928-1954* (New Brunswick: Transaction Books, 1983).

[4] Frank Dikötter, *Mao's Great Famine* (New York: Walker & Co., 2010), x.

[5] Everett F. Harrison, *Romans*, ed. Frank E. Gaebelein and J. D. Douglas, vol. 10 of Expositor's Bible Commentary. Accordance electronic ed. (Grand Rapids: Zondervan, 1977), n.p.

[6] John Hare, "Kant on the Rational Instability of Atheism," Chap. 9, In *God and the Ethics of Belief*, edited by Andrew Chignell and Andrew Dole (New York: Cambridge University Press, 2005), 204-205.

[7] David DeSilva, "Paul and the Stoa: A Comparison," in *Journal of the Evangelical Theological Society* vol. 38, no. 4 (12/01 1995), 562.

[8] Quoted by William A. Durbin, "Negotiating the Boundaries of Science and Religion: The Conversion of Allan Sandage," *Zygon* vol. 38 no. 1 (March 2003), 73, http://0-search.ebscohost.com.library.regent.edu/login.aspx?direct=true&db=rfh&AN=ATLA0001348723&site=ehost-live (accessed April 21, 2014).

[9] Ibid, 74.
[10] Quoted in Alister McGrath, *The Passionate Intellect: Christian Faith and the Discipleship of the Mind* (Downers Grove, Ill.: IVP Books, 2006), 72-73.
[11] Peter Frick, "Monotheism and Philosophy: Notes on the Concept of God in Philo and Paul (Romans 1:18-21)," in *Christian Origins and Hellenistic Judaism*, vol. 2, ed. Stanley E. Porter and Andrew W. Pitts (Boston: Brill, 2013), 247.
[12] Dallas Willard, Knowing Christ Today: Why we can Trust Spiritual Knowledge (New York: HarperOne, 2009), 100.
[13] William A. Dembski, "Science and Design," *First Things*, no. 86 (10/01, 1998), 21
[14] Aquinas, n.p.
[15] Richard J. Foster and James Bryan Smith, *Devotional Classics: Selected Readings for Individuals and Groups* (San Francisco: HarperSanFrancisco, 2005), 333.
[16]James R. Edwards, *Romans*, vol. 6 of New International Biblical Commentary. Accordance electronic ed. (Peabody: Hendrickson, 1992), 70-71.
[17] F. F. Bruce, *Romans: An Introduction and Commentary*, vol. 6 of Tyndale New Testament Commentaries. IVP/Accordance electronic ed. (Downers Grove: InterVarsity Press, 1985), 97.
[18]C. S. Lewis, Mere Christianity: A Revised and Amplified Edition, with a New Introduction, of the Three Books, Broadcast Talks, Christian Behaviour, and Beyond Personality, Kindle electronic edition (New York: HarperCollins e-books, 2009), 7.
[19] Ibid, 38.
[20] C. Stephen Evans and R. Zachary Manis, *Philosophy of Religion : Thinking about Faith*. (Downers Grove, Ill.: IVP Academic, 2009), 88-89.

[21] Edgar A. Towne, "John Calvin's Unlikely but Significant Response to Recent Outspoken Atheism," *Encounter* 69, no. 2 (03/01, 2008), 11.
[22] Ibid.
[23] Daniel C. Maguire, "Atheists for Jesus: The Moral Core of Religious Experience," *Christian Century* 110, no. 35 (12/08, 1993),1229.
[24] Francis Collins, The Language of God: A Scientist Present Evidence for Belief (New York: Free Press, 2006).
[25] Ibid, 225.

TEN
THE FIFTH CONVERSATION: WHO WAS JESUS? WHAT DID HE SAY?

A few years ago when I was youth pastoring I took my students to a corn maze. Have you ever been to one of these things? They're a real phenomenon in the northeast United States. Here's how it works—a farmer plants a large field of corn, then around harvest time he carves all kinds of twisting paths in the corn with sharp turns, dead ends, and tricks to help you get lost. Every corn maze has only one entrance and one exit. I had never been to one before, but it seemed like a fun idea, so one Friday night in October we loaded up the church bus and headed to the corn maze. I had no idea what I was in for. It was a crisp cool autumn evening, and we arrived at the Corn Maze about 8pm. We gathered around a campfire and received our instructions. The person in charge of the maze emphasized we needed to get through pretty quickly because they were closing in one hour. "No big deal," I thought to myself. I didn't think we would need much time because, even though they were fun, corn mazes were mostly for kids, so it wouldn't take us too long to find our way out. I was terribly wrong.

We all entered the maze enthusiastically, quickly heading down a few of the various pathways and finding amusement when we took a wrong turn. Little did we know we had entered the mother-of-all corn mazes. We wandered for about 30 minutes before we reached what had been described as a halfway point—a tower bridge that had been constructed in the middle of the maze. By this time it was 8:45pm, and the urgency of completing the puzzle started racing in my mind. The corn maze was closing in 15 minutes, and we needed to get out of here! In addition, I was getting really tired of looking at corn stalks and was ready for a change of scenery. It was dark, it was cold, and even though I knew where I was (in the middle of a corn field), I had no idea how to get out of there. We walked on, around corners and through what appeared to be shortcuts. At 8:55pm we arrived back at the tower bridge. We had wandered for ten minutes, and hadn't gotten anywhere!

A slight panic began to set in as I realized we were walking around in circles and weren't making any progress. All I could see was corn! Row after row, dead end after dead end, I kept moving around in circles. I started to think, "I'm never going to get out of here!" Soon I was ready to break through the corn stalk walls and bust my way out of the maze, but everywhere I turned there was another corn maze worker making sure we obeyed the rules. There was only one way out of the maze, and we couldn't find it! Anxiousness began to creep into my gut, like when you're nervous about something big that's going to happen, and you don't know how it's going to turn out. Forty-five minutes earlier I had been lighthearted and excited, but now I was miserable and ready for this to be over. How could we ever find the way out? There was one path to the exit, and no matter how hard we tried, we couldn't find it! Have I mentioned how much I hate corn mazes?

I'm not sure what gave us away. Maybe the corn maze worker who spotted us could tell from my gaze that I was eyeing up the corn stalks to see where I could break through to freedom. Maybe they saw the anxiety written all over my face as I thought about being stuck in a corn maze for life. Maybe they realized we weren't having fun anymore. Or maybe it was quitting time and they wanted to get out of the maze as badly as I did. I'm not sure what drove that worker to ask the question, but I'm sure glad she did. See, as a man, I don't like to ask for directions—I like to figure it out for myself. But I couldn't figure it out for myself—I was helpless. So, even though I was slightly embarrassed, I was also grateful when the worker asked, "Do you need help finding the way out?" She pointed us in the right direction, and it didn't take long for us to find our way to the exit and to freedom.

The Maze of Sin

Have you ever felt this way about life? Like you're walking around in a maze and can't find the way out? It wouldn't surprise me if you did, because I know I have. Life can be like a maze, and when it comes to sin, we can really get lost in all the twists and turns. The same thing is true for our friends. The search for meaning, purpose, and redemption from the maze of sin can really get someone turned around if he doesn't know the way out. I've known a lot of people who've searched for redemption in a lot of dead ends; alcoholism, sexual promiscuity, marriage and divorce, money, good looks, competition, careers. You may be too young to personally know anyone like this, but you probably have at least one friend whose life has been damaged by someone else's failed attempt to get out of the maze, often by a parent or sibling. We have an opportunity to help people out of the crazy maze of sin, and we know how to solve this great puzzle: Jesus is the only path out of sin's maze, and we are the ones who are pointing people in His direction.

Jesus is the only path out of sin's maze, and we are the ones who are pointing people in His direction.

In his letter to the young church planter Titus, Paul said that God's grace has appeared, bringing with it salvation for all people, and that Titus was to declare these things with authority (Titus 2:11,15). Then he reminded Titus that all of us who know God were once lost in the maze of sin, "For we ourselves were once foolish, disobedient, led astray, slaves to various passions and pleasures, passing our days in malice and envy, hated by others and hating one another" (3:3 ESV). But when we were at our most despairing point in the maze, the "goodness and loving kindness of God our Savior appeared," and "He saved us" (3:4-5 ESV). Just as we were directed to the path out of the sin maze through Jesus Christ, we now get to help others find that same path. We are God's workers in the maze of sin and life, pointing people to the only exit—Jesus Christ.

We Need to Talk About Jesus

We must connect our friends to the Truth of who Jesus is. By asking about their story, we met their need to be heard and became friends. By asking them about their interests, we demonstrated that we cared about them. By delving into their hopes and dreams, we showed that we care about their future. By pointing them to the Dream Giver, we pointed them to eternity. But it is not enough to leave people on the slope of genuine friendship, to arouse their curiosity about God, and not to lead them to the top of the mountain where Jesus is. Rather, we must continue to take them up to Jesus. We must lead them to the foot of the cross and allow them to make a choice. This may be a challenging conversation to have, but you need to talk about the Gospel if you want it to be heard.

That's what Paul meant when he wrote, "'Everyone who calls on the name of the Lord will be saved.' How, then, can they call on the one they have not believed in? And how can they believe in the one of whom they have not heard? And how can they hear without someone preaching to them?" (Romans 10:13–14 NIV). A lot of people think if they are a good person, serve others, and love God; their friends will eventually come to know Jesus. But that is not a Biblical principle! The truth is, almost no one comes to Jesus without being told about Him. Scripture declares this plainly, "Consequently, faith comes from hearing the message, and the message is heard through the word about Christ" (10:17 NIV). At some point, you need to have a conversation about Jesus.

This may be a challenging conversation to have, but you need to talk about the Gospel if you want it to be heard.

Having the Conversation

Every good conversation begins and flows with good questions. Here are some questions to get you going, but you can always develop your own and allow the conversation to flow naturally:

- ***Who do you think Jesus was?*** There are only a few answers to this question; he was a good man, he was the Son of God, he was crazy, he was a liar, he was a prophet. The important thing is to get your friend thinking about who Jesus is, or was. If he answers by saying, "He was

God's Son," or "He was a prophet," follow up by asking, *"So what does that mean for us today? How should our lives be impacted by His life?"*

- ***Do you think faith in Jesus helps or hurts someone?*** Depending on your friend's perspective, the answer to this question could go either way. By asking this question you're doing two things: (1) you are getting him to think about how faith could be a benefit, and (2) you are opening the door to share why faith in Jesus has helped you. Follow up by asking, *"Do you think faith in Jesus could help you in any way?"*
- ***Was Jesus the Son of God?*** This is a more direct way of asking about Jesus' nature. Your friend will have to directly answer your question. Follow up with, *"Why?"* or *"Why not?"* and, *"So what does that mean for us today?"*
- ***What do you think Jesus meant when he said…?*** This can lead into a variety of questions that you can formulate and think through using Jesus' actual words. By asking your friend directly what she thinks about Jesus' exact words, you are confronting her with Jesus' own statements about himself. Jesus made waves in his day by the things He said, and you have the potential to make waves in the life of your friend by getting her to ponder Jesus' words in her life. In the following section, there are 12 statements Jesus made about himself that can help you have twelve different conversations about Him.

What Jesus Said About Himself

Jesus said many things about Himself. In fact, John wrote that He said and did so much, that there probably weren't enough books in the world at that time to write it all down. It's impossible to contain everything that Jesus said in one chapter, so we'll focus on several of Jesus' "I am" statements. These are some of the things Jesus said about Himself in the Gospels.

I am eternal (John 8:58). One day in a conversation with some devout Jews, called Pharisees, Jesus was talking about

Abraham. The Pharisees were challenging a lot of what Jesus had been saying, and they were trying to trap Him in blasphemy so they could have Him put to death. Jesus said, "I tell you the truth, before Abraham was born, *I am*!" He used a very specific set of words to make this statement. By saying, "I am," Jesus was using the same words God used to introduce himself to Moses during the burning bush experience. When Moses asked who the voice in the burning bush was, the reply was, "I am that I am." Jesus was saying that He was God, and by using Abraham's existence in his statement, He was saying, "I am eternal." Jesus had no beginning and no end, which is also stated in the Old Testament verses of Psalm 90:1-2, 102:12, and Isaiah 57:15. When Jesus described himself with the title "I am" he expressed that He always was and always will be. As your friend, *"Do you think Jesus really was God? Do you think He's been around since before time began?"*

I am gentle and humble (Matthew 11:29). What do you think of when you think of God? A lot of people think of God as a mean old man, sitting in heaven and waiting to hit people who break His rules over the head with a giant club. But Jesus said this about Himself, "I am gentle and humble in heart." By talking about Jesus' gentleness and humility, you talk about the kind of person people are comfortable being around. Help your friend understand who Jesus really is by talking about these traits of His being. Jesus is powerful; all of creation was made by Him and through Him, and when He walked the earth He worked many miracles and healings. He had great authority, but He was kind and gentle, humble and loving. Isn't that the kind of person you want to be around?

In Jesus' day, the culture around Israel was very Greek, because the Greeks had ruled over the region, followed by the Romans, who embraced Greek culture. Greek writers thought gentleness and humbleness were good qualities, as long as they weren't found in rulers and powerful citizens.[1] The ruling class of society wanted to be seen as powerful, and they could only accept humility and gentleness as good qualities among the poor. Jesus' statement is surrounded by interactions with the Pharisees, who opposed Jesus and tried to use their authority to discredit Him. The Gospels point out the pride, love for power and position, and pronounced authority the Pharisees showed in their daily activities (Matthew 23:5-12). By making this statement when He did, Jesus was declaring that He was different from the other religious people—He was all-powerful, but He was also humble and gentle. Ask your friend, *"Can God be humble? If Jesus was all-powerful, why was He so gentle? How is that possible?"*

I am a servant (Luke 22:27). During the last supper, just before His death, Jesus was sitting around a table with His disciples eating dinner and teaching them. There were also servants in the room—waiters who were bringing the food and making sure everything was going smoothly. Jesus asked the questions, "Who is the greater, one who reclines at table or one who serves? Is it not the one who reclines at table?" Then he pointed out, "I am among you as the one who serves." Again, Jesus goes out of His way to show that He, being God, is a servant to man. The disciples would have had this idea fresh in their minds, because during this same dinner, Jesus had washed His disciples' feet. The word Jesus used to describe "one who serves" is the same word (in Greek) for table waiter. Jesus was making it very clear that He was a servant. Ask your friend, *"How did Jesus serve the world?"*

I am the bread of life (John 6:35). I love bread, especially when it's grilled up with cheese between the slices! Jesus talked about food, particularly bread, to make a point about Himself. Bread was a main food item in the middle-eastern diet. In Scripture, it's also symbolic of all the food that man needs to live. Jesus said, "I am the bread of life; whoever comes to me shall not hunger, and whoever believes in me shall never thirst." He was saying He was spiritual food that gives sustaining life. Just as important, when He talks about meeting hunger and thirst eternally, it is on the condition that we come to Him. In other words, Jesus only satisfies our spiritual hunger and thirst if we walk away from our old lives completely and come to Him to meet our needs. Jesus also used food to talk about Himself during the Last Supper, when He said His body was the bread and His blood was the wine. Ask your friend, *"Have you ever been spiritually hungry or curious? In what ways does Jesus meet the hunger and thirst of those who follow Him?"*

I am the light of the world (John 8:12). Have you ever found yourself in a very dark room? Or have you ever been at home when the power went out at night? It's amazing how complicated life can become when you don't have light to show you where things are. Stuff you use everyday can suddenly become hard to find because you don't have light to show you the way. When I wake up early in the morning I don't want to turn the light on, because I don't want to wake up my wife. But I can't find my clothes in the dark, so I often use my cellphone as a flashlight. Have you ever done that? It's amazing how much difference even the smallest light can make. Did you know that it's impossible to have life without light? No plants would grow, no heat would exist, and life couldn't happen without light.

Jesus said, "I am the light of the world. Whoever follows me will not walk in darkness, but will have the light of life." It's important to understand where Jesus was, and what was happening, when He said that. Jesus was in Jerusalem during the Feast of Tabernacles, one of the historic Jewish festivals that was still being honored during Jesus' day. During the Feast of Tabernacles, four large golden lamps were lit in the temple at Jerusalem. The lamps were big enough to rise over the Temple walls, and were said to illuminate the city of Jerusalem during the festival.[2] The lights affected the entire city, and burned for days at a time. By the end of the festival, the lights gradually went out until just one remained burning—a symbol that the Israelites were waiting for their salvation. This is when Jesus declared Himself to be that salvation—the light of the world, the salvation of all mankind. Ask your friend, *"How does light help us? In what ways was Jesus a light in His generation?*

In what ways does He provide light for us now?"

I am the door (John 10:9). Jesus was using the illustration of sheep and shepherds to teach his disciples in John 10. He said, "I am the door. If anyone enters by me, he will be saved and will go in and out and find pasture." In ancient times, especially in Greek writings, people often thought about entering the afterlife through a gate or a doorway.[3] Jesus was saying that He was the gate to heaven, and that if anyone wanted to get to heaven, he had to go through Him. Anyone who enters through Jesus will be saved for all eternity from sin, and find peace and spiritual nourishment. Ask your friend, *"In what way is Jesus the door? How does going through Jesus save anybody? What does it mean to 'find pasture'?"*

I am the Good Shepherd (John 10:11). Just two verses later, Jesus refers to Himself as the Good Shepherd. What's a good shepherd do? He lays down his life for the sheep. Instead of the sheep suffering for their missteps – for instance, wandering into the path of a wolf – the shepherd steps to their defense and accepts the consequences. Jesus was willing to die for us, His sheep, and accept the punishment for our sins. It was His death on the cross that rescued us from eternal consequences. Most shepherds wouldn't die for their sheep, and if it were to happen, it would likely be an accident. Jesus declares that He is different—willing to die so that we may know life. Ask your friend, *"In what ways was Jesus the Good Shepherd? Why did we need Him to die for us? Why is someone laying down their life for someone else considered heroic and good?"*

I am the Christ, Son of the Blessed One (Mark 14:61-62). Jesus was asked by the High Priest in Jerusalem, "Are you the Christ, the Son of the Blessed One?" He answered, "I am. And you will see the Son of Man sitting at the right hand of the Mighty One and coming on the clouds of heaven." Jesus declared that He was the Messiah who would save Israel, and even the whole earth, from sin. We need to declare it as well! Not only did Jesus say that He was the Messiah in this verse, but also that He was the One prophesied about in Daniel 7:13-14, "coming with the clouds of Heaven...given authority, glory and sovereign power; all peoples, nations and men of every language worshiped him." Jesus was not just talking about His coming death, but also about the day when He would return to earth in the clouds. On that day, He will take all the believers on earth, those who live and even those who have died, to heaven with Him. Ask your friend, *"What does it mean to be 'the Christ'? Why do we need a Savior?"*

I am the resurrection and the life (John 11:25). Jesus had a friend named Lazarus, whose sisters were Mary and Martha. Lazarus died and was buried in the tomb for four days before Jesus arrived in their hometown. Martha went out to meet Jesus on the road. She was upset that He wasn't there to save Lazarus from dying. Jesus told her that Lazarus would rise again, but she thought He was talking about the last days. He said, "I am the resurrection and the life. Whoever believes in me will live, even though he dies; and whoever lives and believes in me will never die. Do you believe this?" Then Jesus went to Lazarus' tomb and raised him from the dead. He demonstrated His power over death by raising His friend from the grave, and later by rising from the dead Himself.

As Christians, it's likely that we will face death one day, unless Jesus comes back to earth in our lifetime. But we can be assured, even though we die, we will live—free from death forever. We will physically die, but we continue to spiritually live. For someone who doesn't believe in God, death may be considered the end. But for the Christian, it is only the beginning. You can ask your friend a lot of great questions here, like, *"What do you think happens when we die? What do you think happened to Lazarus during those four days? How can we live, even though we die? Do you feel good about what is going to happen to you after death?"*

I am the way, the truth, and the life (John 14:6). Just like there was only one exit to the Corn Maze, Jesus is the only way to salvation. He said, "I am the way, and the truth, and the life. No one comes to the Father except through me." It's never been popular—certainly not today—to claim there is only one way to God, but that is what Jesus said in His own words, and it is the truth. He is the way—the only way—to God. The people who were around Jesus, and the Christians in the first 100 years after His death, even called Christianity "the Way" (Acts 9:2; 19:9, 23; 24:14, 22). Jesus was God's perfect Son, and only His death, His sacrifice, would make a way for us to be connected to God. Peter said the same thing in Acts 4:12, "Salvation is found in no one else, for there is no other name under heaven given to men by which we must be saved." Ask your friend, *"What is it about Jesus' life that makes Him 'the way' to God? Why did Jesus say no one could come to God except through Him? Do you believe Jesus is the way to God?"*

I am the vine (John 15:5). Have you ever seen a grape vineyard? It looks like there are a lot of plants in a row, and they are connected to a wire, like a fence, that keeps the vines and branches off the ground. In reality there are only a few plants on each row, but it looks like there are a lot. That's because each plant can stretch across the wire fencing for up to 100 feet and produce many grapes. In this verse, Jesus refers to Himself as the vine, saying, "I am the vine; you are the branches. Whoever abides in me and I in him, he it is that bears much fruit, for apart from me you can do nothing." When someone turns his or her life over to Christ, it's not just a one-time deal. It is a commitment of the whole-person for a life-change. This is important to understand, because if you are able to talk to a friend about Jesus, it can change his or her life forever. In fact, a healthy vine should produce good fruit. On the contrary, if we become cut off from God, we can't produce any fruit, for He is the source of life. Ask your friend, *"Can a branch survive when it's cut off from the vine? If Jesus is the vine, and His followers are branches, what kind of fruit should they produce?"*

I am going to the Father (John 16:28). This conversation can help you explain why Jesus resurrected and then left the earth. He said, "I came from the Father and have come into the world, and now I am leaving the world and going to the Father." Jesus physical presence on the earth was temporary and purposeful; he became the sacrifice necessary to make all of us reconciled to God. He came from God the Father in Heaven, and once His work was done He returned to God the Father in Heaven. Jesus was one of the most famous people to walk the face of the earth. You can even visit His tomb in Jerusalem, but it is empty. It was empty when the Gospels were first written, too, because Jesus completed his work and returned to God. Ask your friend, *"What was the most important thing Jesus did before leaving the earth? Jesus is so famous, but his grave has always been empty. Why is that?"*

Can All of This Be True?

It will be natural for your friend to have doubts about Jesus. It will be normal for them to be skeptical, and to ask a lot of questions. Sometimes the best way to answer a question is with a question. C.S. Lewis came to a conclusion about Jesus in his book *Mere Christianity*, that can help you ask your friends some powerful questions about the truth of Jesus' statements. He wrote:

> I am trying here to prevent anyone saying the really foolish thing that people often say about Him: I'm ready to accept Jesus as a great moral teacher, but I don't accept his claim to be God. That is the one thing we must not say. A man who was merely a man and said the sort of things Jesus said would not be a great moral teacher. He would either be a lunatic — on the level with the man who says he is a poached egg — or else he would be the Devil of Hell. You must make your choice. Either this man was, and is, the Son of God, or else a madman or something worse. You can shut him up for a fool, you can spit at him and kill him as a demon or you can fall at his feet and call him Lord and God, but let us not come with any patronizing nonsense about his being a great human teacher. He has not left that open to us. He did not intend to...Now it seems to me obvious that He was neither a lunatic nor a fiend: and consequently, however strange or terrifying or unlikely it may seem, I have to accept the view that He was and is God.[4]

Lewis' argument has come to be known as the "Liar, Lunatic, or Lord" question. Sometimes it's also referred to as, "Mad, Bad, or God." If you've had some good conversations with your friends about who Jesus was and what He said, you can move them to a point of decision by using this discussion.

Jesus said a lot of controversial things that cannot be accepted as being "good" unless they were true. For example, He said he could forgive people of their sins (Mark 2:7). The teachers of the law were outraged when they heard this and said, "He's blaspheming! Who can forgive sins but God alone?" They had made their conclusion; He was either a liar or a lunatic. Jesus said that he existed before Abraham, that he was sent from God His Father and was going back to God. He claimed He would come back to judge the world at the end of time (Matthew 25:31-33). How can anyone say these things and still be a good person, unless what they are saying is true? Imagine someone in your school making these claims—you would call them crazy, deeply disturbed, or think they were running some kind of scam to manipulate people—a truly evil thing to do. But Jesus was taken seriously, not just by those who followed Him, but by the authorities of His day. They knew He wasn't crazy. Explain this to your friend, and then ask the question, *"So which is it? Was Jesus crazy? Was he just a liar? Or was it true? Is He the Lord? And if so, what does that mean for you?"*

Who Do You Say That He Is?

One day Jesus and his disciples were walking towards the villages at Caesarea Philippi (Mark 8:27-30) when Jesus asked them, "Who do people say I am?" The disciples answered, "Some say John the Baptist; others say Elijah; and still others, one the prophets." It was Peter who spoke up and said, "You are the Christ, the Son of the Living God." It was this same Peter who spoke a powerful sermon on the day the Church was founded in Acts 2, stating, "God has raised this Jesus to life, and we are all witnesses of the fact. Exalted to the right hand of God, he has received from the Father the promised Holy Spirit and has poured out what you now see and hear...Repent and be baptized, every one of you, in the name of Jesus Christ for the forgiveness of your sins. And you will receive the gift of the Holy Spirit" (Acts 2:32–33, 38 NIV). On that day, about 3,000 people repented and accepted that Christ was the Savior and Lord. Peter told the crowd who Jesus was out of his own experience. Peter told Christ's story, but it was also Peter's story.

There will be no greater witness for Jesus than your story of who Jesus is. Who do you say Jesus is? Did Jesus change your life? Has Jesus given you new purpose and meaning? Does Jesus give you the sense of personal fulfillment that much of the world desires? You need to talk about who Jesus is to you, not just who Jesus was in the Bible or to the disciples. Ask yourself that question—and then write down the answers. This

> There will be no greater witness for Jesus than your story of who Jesus is.

is the beginning of a powerful answer to the powerful question that could demonstrate a powerful witness to your friends.

Prayer

Throughout this chapter we've reviewed different ways of talking to your friends about Jesus. Now begin to pray for God to help you commit these questions and conversations to memory. Ask God to give you an opportunity to speak with your friends about Jesus. Ponder the question, "Who is Jesus to me?" and ask God to help you formulate a powerful answer that can show your friends the real Jesus. Pray for your friends personally, by name, and ask God to show them Jesus through their daily experiences, and through your life.

---

[1] Craig S. Keener, *The IVP Bible Background Commentary: New Testament*, Accordance electronic ed. (Downers Grove: InterVarsity Press, 1993), n.p.

[2] Andreas J. Köstenberger, "John," in *John, Acts*, vol. 2 of *Zondervan Illustrated Bible Backgrounds Commentary: New Testament*. ed. Clinton E. Arnold; Accordance electronic ed. (Grand Rapids: Zondervan, 2002), 82.

[3] Ibid, 100.

[4] Lewis, *Mere Christianity*, 52.

ELEVEN
WRAPPING UP
THE GOSPEL, APOLOGIES, PERFECTION, AND OTHER STUFF

My wife and I went on a 7-night cruise recently. Every night we sat around a large table with four other couples at dinner. They were all young and mostly newlyweds, and even though my wife and I aren't *that* old, we were the oldest couple in the group. Each night I engaged one of the conversations in this book in one way or another. I was experimenting with powerful questions, and testing how long it would take us to start talking about God. There were 10 of us around the table and the conversations went pretty slowly because everybody had something to say. I didn't mind the pace of the conversation, because it was a pleasure just getting to know everybody.

Usually everyone would gather for dinner and spend some time discussing the events of the day and their experiences on the cruise. Inevitably, the conversation would get stuck on small talk and an awkward pause would ensue. That's when I would ask a powerful question, and the next 45-60 minutes would be filled with conversation as each person or couple went around the table talking about themselves. Simple questions like, "How did you all meet and fall in love? Tell me about your family. What do you like to? What are you passionate about? Tell me more about that. What would you do if you could do anything?" And 10 people spent two hours each night talking, listening, and learning about one another. That's 14 hours of meaningful conversation between people who previously didn't know each other!

For the first night I hardly said anything, I just asked the questions and listened. It's amazing how the right question can generate discussion. The second night they started to turn the questions back on me. "Hey, you never told us what you were passionate about? What do you do?" Of course I shared about my faith, my job as a minister, and my passion for the Gospel. Everyone listened closely, and because we had already had some great conversations, no one thought it was awkward when my faith came into the conversation. The third, fourth, and fifth nights continued with conversations that didn't seem naturally God-centered. Yet somehow, each night, God came into the discussion, probably because they all knew I was passionate about the Lord.

It's amazing how the right question can generate discussion.

I listened as each couple inevitably shared about their own faith, their perspective of God, and their interactions with the church. I didn't even have to push hard for the information; they mostly volunteered it as we got to know each other better. On the fifth and sixth nights, I felt I'd earned the right to be heard well enough to ask some more direct questions about God and Jesus. By the end of the seventh night I'd had a meaningful conversation about God, Jesus, or the church with every couple around the table.

I've been on a few cruises, and usually the conversation around the dinner table between strangers is awkward, and can even be uncomfortable. At the end of each cruise it's normal to say goodbye and expect to never see the people you had dinner with again. On the last night of this cruise, something happened that I'd not experienced before. Everyone at the table was connected through the conversations we had, and all of them wanted to exchange information so we could keep in touch. We left the ship the next day, and soon Facebook friend invites starting showing up. Some of them even said, "I really enjoyed talking to you about God. Can I stay in touch with you? Can we talk about this some more?"

The conversations and principles in this book are powerful and can help you develop relationships that will connect others with Jesus. They take practice, and they take time, but they pay off in ways that many evangelistic methods don't. I'd never met the couples at my dinner table on the cruise before, but we starting having conversations about God on our second night together. That's amazing! By the end of the week, we had established relationships strong enough to talk meaningfully about faith and laid down a foundation for future discussions. Through practice, time, and investment, you can do the same with people you encounter and want to share your faith with. There are just a few more ideas I want to share with you as this book wraps up.

Explaining the Gospel

So, you've had a great conversation with a few people and they want to know more about the Gospel, or you've earned the right to be heard and you feel like it's time to share the Gospel. What's the best way to explain it? Hopefully your conversations have already paved the way for this, and your friend already has a grasp of God's existence and your faith in Him, but it's still important to explain the Gospel simply. This is actually pretty easy to do, because the Gospel is easy to understand. The hardest part about sharing your faith is earning the right to be heard by developing meaningful relationships through conversation, so you've already done the hard part. At this point, sharing the Gospel should be a natural step in your friendship.

There are lots of ways to explain the Gospel. I've developed a three point explanation that's abbreviated GMC, so it's easy to remember:

1. **G**od exists and created mankind. He is holy and desires to have connection with man. Man is ultimately fulfilled and content when connected to God, the Creator.
2. **M**an's sin disconnected us from God. Reconnection to God can only be achieved through a selfless and worthy sacrifice that makes up for the harm of sin.
3. **C**hrist is God's son and came to the earth to be the sacrifice, taking on the price of our sin so that we could be reconnected to God. Everyone must come to God in faith and live a life of faith, which results in earthly contentedness and eternal life.

There are many great methods for explaining the Gospel, and you may find one that's easier to remember than others. One of my favorites is the *Dare2Share* model called "Life in Six Words."[1] It uses the word "Gospel" to help you remember the six words, which are **G**od **O**ur **S**ins **P**aying **E**veryone **L**ife. Each word stands for one element of the Gospel story. For more information on that model, see www.LifeIn6Words.com. Another favorite of mine is "The Bridge Card," which is available through www.MyHealthyChurch.com. The Bridge Card gives an illustration of the Gospel in a picture format, and supplies scripture references on the back for you to use. In the Bridge illustration, sin creates a chasm between God and man, and the Cross creates a bridge over the chasm so we can be reconnected to God. Again, any of these models are good; just find the one that works best for you.

> The hardest part about sharing your faith is earning the right to be heard by developing meaningful relationships through conversation, so you've already done the hard part.

Scriptures for Explaining the Gospel

Memorizing and using Scripture is even more important than a good model for sharing the Gospel. All of the following Scriptures are helpful, and can be used with the GMC method, or many of the others:

Romans 3:21-26 NIV

But now a righteousness from God, apart from law, has been made known, to which the Law and the Prophets testify. This righteousness from God comes through faith in Jesus Christ to all who believe. There is no difference, for all have sinned and fall short of the glory of God, and are justified freely by his grace through the redemption that came by Christ Jesus. God presented him as a sacrifice of atonement, through faith in his blood. He did this to demonstrate his justice, because in his forbearance he had left the sins committed beforehand unpunished— he did it to demonstrate his justice at the present time, so as to be just and the one who justifies those who have faith in Jesus.

Romans 6:20-23 NIV

"When you were slaves to sin, you were free from the control of righteousness. What benefit did you reap at that time from the things you are now ashamed of? Those things result in death! But now that you have been set free from sin and have become slaves to God, the benefit you reap leads to holiness, and the result is eternal life. For the wages of sin is death, but the gift of God is eternal life in Christ Jesus our Lord."

Memorizing Scripture is even more important than a good model for sharing the Gospel.

John 3:16-18 NIV

""For God so loved the world that he gave his one and only Son, that whoever believes in him shall not perish but have eternal life. For God did not send his Son into the world to condemn the world, but to save the world through him. Whoever believes in him is not condemned, but whoever does not believe stands condemned already because he has not believed in the name of God's one and only Son."

John 3:3 NIV

"Jesus declared, "I tell you the truth, no one can see the kingdom of God unless he is born again.'""

John 14:6 NIV

"Jesus answered, "I am the way and the truth and the life. No one comes to the Father except through me."

Romans 10:9-13 NIV

"That if you confess with your mouth, "Jesus is Lord," and believe in your heart that God raised him from the dead, you will be saved. For it is with your heart that you believe and are justified, and it is with your mouth that you confess and are saved. As the Scripture says, "Anyone who trusts in him will never be put to shame." For there is no difference between Jew and Gentile—the same Lord is Lord of all and richly blesses all who call on him, for, "Everyone who calls on the name of the Lord will be saved.""

2 Corinthians 5:14-15 NIV

"For Christ's love compels us, because we are convinced that one died for all, and therefore all died. And he died for all, that those who live should no longer live for themselves but for him who died for them and was raised again."

Revelation 3:20 NIV

"Here I am! I stand at the door and knock. If anyone hears my voice and opens the door, I will come in and eat with him, and he with me."

Coming to Jesus

Coming to Jesus is as simple as prayer, and you may need to help your friend pray if it's their first time. Scripture makes it clear that anyone who confesses that "Jesus is Lord" with their mouth, while believing in their heart that God raised Him from the dead, will be saved. It's simple, so the prayer can be simple too:

> God, I believe that Jesus died for my sins and that you raised him from the dead. I confess that Jesus is Lord of my life. I repent of my sins, and I commit myself to you in faith.

Making Apologies

One of the most important skills you'll need when sharing your faith is knowing how to apologize. Jesus was gentle and humble, and humility is often demonstrated through an apology. There's a good chance you'll offend someone at some point. That's okay. Just apologize and ask for their forgiveness. You will likely make the mistake of pushing your message too hard and pushing your friend away. Just apologize and ask for their forgiveness. Look for another opportunity when you've earned the right to be heard again.

> There's a good chance you'll need to apologize at some point.

An apology may be in order if you've been friends with someone for a long time but have never shared the Gospel. As Will McRaney stated, "A direct and honest approach is helpful in this situation."[2] Explain that you are sorry, because even though you've been good friends, you haven't really talked about what's most important to you in life. When you're honest and humble enough to apologize, your message is much more likely to be received.

The Myth of Perfection

For some reason Christians often think they need to be morally perfect in order to serve God correctly. To make matters worse, many often pretend they're perfect, and all of us are far from it. Being a Christian is not about being perfect, it's about being forgiven. When you make serving God about being morally perfect, you make it hard for most people to come to Jesus, because they know they can't be morally perfect. You also misrepresent what the Gospel is all about. Additionally, most people can see right through this myth of perfection, and they'd rather be honest than be a hypocrite who pretends to be perfect.

Don't pretend to be something you're not. Don't pretend to be perfect. Let's be very honest with ourselves—there's only been one perfect person in the history of the world—Jesus Christ. If you pretend that you are also perfect, you're putting yourself on a pedestal to be glorified instead of glorifying Jesus. It's like setting ourselves on the same playing field with Jesus; Jesus was perfect, and so are we. Nothing could be further from the truth. The Apostle Paul, who wrote two-thirds of the New Testament, said that he was the chief of all sinners. If Paul said that about himself, how much more so are we imperfect in our actions and living?

> Don't pretend to be something you're not. Don't pretend to be perfect.

One of the great challenges of pretending to be perfect is the inevitable slip-up. Everyone sins and everyone fails, and perfection won't be attainable until Jesus returns and perfects us Himself. If you pretend Christianity is about being morally perfect, you'll look pretty silly the next time you mess up, and you'll make the Gospel look false. Instead of pretending to be perfect, just be honest and admit that you're imperfect and forgiven. If you mess up and your friends know it, try apologizing. If you lied and your friends know it, just say, "I'm really sorry I lied. That doesn't represent Jesus at all. That's just more proof why I need Him in my life."

I knew a student who made a commitment to represent God as a missionary to his school campus. He sincerely loved the Lord and wanted to make God's glory known. But he wasn't perfect. In a moment of weakness he went to a party and tried marijuana. It was the first and last time he did anything like it. The hardest part about it was the public nature of his mistake. Everyone knew he was a Christian, and everyone knew he tried pot. He felt terrible, not just about his sin, but about being a poor example for the Gospel. He started getting made fun of, because he had pretended to be a "good Christian," but he turned out to be less than what he had projected himself to be.

Then he did something amazing—he owned his mistake and his sin nature. He started apologizing to his friends for his error and for his poor representation of Jesus. He started exclaiming that his need for Jesus was demonstrated through his weakness, and everyone else's need is demonstrated through theirs as well. Soon he was back on mission—proclaiming the Gospel and inviting friends to church and to Christ. His humility in weakness made it possible for his friends to come to Jesus. Your humility paves the way for your friends to accept Jesus, as well. But if you're arrogant and prideful, refusing to acknowledge your

> Your humility paves the way for your friends to accept Jesus.

own faults and weaknesses, you are living a lie. In doing so, you're not acknowledging a need for Jesus at all. You are likely blocking someone from coming to Christ.

No Guilt, No Shame

Finally, if you've earned the right to be heard, had the conversations, shared your faith, and shared the Gospel, you've done your part. At the end of the day, your friend will either accept Jesus now, later, or not at all. Pray for them, cry for them, continue to talk to them, but do not feel guilt or shame if they don't accept Christ. It's our job to proclaim the Gospel, but it's their choice to accept it. And the reality is we don't save people; Jesus does. If we've been faithful to our duties of proclamation, God will honor our efforts and not waste them. Saving people is God's business, and we get to be used by Him in the process. But in the end, *we* don't save anyone, God does.

> We don't save people; Jesus does.

I hope this book has helped you realize the importance of conversation in sharing the Gospel, and helped you become a better conversationalist along the way. I pray that God will help you to begin having powerful conversations, develop meaningful relationships, and connect people with Jesus. I pray the Holy Spirit will speak to you, help you to discover how He is drawing your friends to God, and give you boldness to ask powerful questions. I pray that you throw off all that hinders you, including sin that entangles you, that you run with perseverance, fix your eyes upon Jesus, and remember His suffering so that you do not grow weary and lose heart (Hebrews 12:1-3). So...what are you waiting for? Go out and initiate powerful conversations that lead to Jesus!

---

[1] www.lifein6words.com
[2] McRaney, 135.

BIBLIOGRAPHY

Aristides. *The Apology of Aristides the Philosopher*. The Ante-Nicene Fathers: Translations of the Writings of the Fathers Down to A.D. 325. Edited by Allan Menzies. Accordance electronic ed. ed. Vol. X. Grand Rapids: Wm. B. Eerdmans, 1951.

Bright, Bill. *Witnessing without Fear: How to Share Your Faith with Confidence*. San Bernardino, California: Here's Life Publishers, 1987.

Comiskey, Joel, Sam Scaggs, and Ben Wong. *You can Coach: How to Help Leaders Build Healthy Churches through Coaching*. Moreno Valley, CA: CCS Publishing, 2010.

Dikötter, Frank. *Mao's Great Famine: The History of China's Devastating Catastrophe, 1958-1962*. New York: Walker & Co., 2010.

Durbin, William A. "Negotiating the Boundaries of Science and Religion: The Conversion of Allan Sandage." *Zygon* 38, no. 1 (03/01, 2003): 71-84.

Dyadkin, Iosif G. *Unnatural Deaths in the USSR, 1928-1954*. New Brunswick: Transaction Books, 1983.

Fay, William. *Share Jesus without Fear*. Nashville: Broadman & Holman Publishers, 1999.

Galli, Mark. "Speak the Gospel. use Deeds when Necessary." Christianity Today. http://www.christianitytoday.com/ct/2009/mayweb-only/120-42.0.html?paging=off (accessed June 24, 2014).

Gaub, Ken. *What's Your Passion? Proven Tips for Witnessing to Anyone, Anytime, Anywhere*. Green Forest, AR: New Leaf Press, 2004.

Green, Michael. *Sharing Your Faith with Friends and Family: Talking about Jesus without Offending*. Grand Rapids: Baker Books, 2005.

———. *One to One: How to Share Your Faith with a Friend*. Nashville: Moorings, 1995.

Henderson, Jim. *A.k.a. "LOST": Discovering Ways to Connect with the People Jesus Misses most*. Colorado Springs: WaterBrook Press, 2005.

Hibberd, James. "'the Walking Dead': How to Comprehend its Massive Ratings." Entertainment Weekly. http://insidetv.ew.com/2013/11/11/the-walking-dead-ratings/ (accessed April 21, 2014).

Hunter III, George G. *The Celtic Way of Evanglism: How Christianity can Reach the West...again*. Nashville: Abingdon Press, 2000.

Innes, Dick. *I Hate Witnessing: A Handbook for Effective Christian Communication*. Upland, California: Acts Communications, 1995.

Jones, E. Stanley. *The Christ of the Indian Road*. New York: Grosset & Dunlap Publishers, 1935.

Jones, Scott J. *The Evangelistic Love of God & Neighbor: A Theology of Witness & Discipleship*. Nashville: Abingdon Press, 2003.

Kallenberg, Brad J. *Live to Tell: Evangelism for a Postmodern Age*. Grand Rapids: Brazos Press, 2002.

Knibbs, Kate. "Instagram Grows Faster than Facebook, Twitter, Says Survey." Digital Trends. http://www.digitaltrends.com/social-media/instagram-is-growing-faster-than-twitter-facebook-and-pinterest-combined-in-2013/#!CGmjd (accessed April 3, 2014).

Köstenberger, Andreas J. *John*. Zondervan Illustrated Bible Backgrounds Commentary. Edited by Clinton E. Arnold. Accordance electronic ed. Vol. 2. Grand Rapids: Zondervan, 2002.

Lansdown, Gerison. *Every Child's Right to be Heard*. Adobe PDF eBook ed. London: Save the Children UK, 2011.

Marche, Stephen. "Why Zombies are Everywhere Now." Esquire. http://www.esquire.com/blogs/culture/why-zombies-are-everywhere (accessed April 21, 2014).

McRaney Jr, Will. *The Art of Personal Evangelism: Sharing Jesus in a Changing Culture*. Nashville: Broadman & Holman Publishers, 2003.

Muyskens, James L. *The Sufficiency of Hope: The Conceptual Foundations of Religion*. Philadelphia: Temple University Press, 1979.

Oliver, Robert T. *Conversation: The Development and Expression of Personality*. Springfield, IL: Charles C. Thomas, 1961.

Peel, William Carr and Walt Larimore. *Going Public with Your Faith: Becoming a Spiritual Influence at Work*. Grand Rapids: Zondervan, 2003.

Petersen, Jim. *Living Proof: Sharing the Gospel Naturally*. Colorado Springs: NavPress, 1989.

Pippert, Rebecca Manley. *Out of the Saltshaker & into the World: Evangelism as a Way of Life*. Downers Grove: InverVarsity Press, 1979.

Poe, Harry Lee. *Christian Witness in a Postmodern World*. Nashville: Abingdon Press, 2001.

Pritchard, G. A. *Willow Creek Seeker Services: Evaluating a New Way of Doing Church*. Grand Rapids, Mich.: Baker Books, 1996.

Richardson, Rick. *Evangelism Outside the Box: New Ways to Help People Experience the Good News*. Downers Grove, Ill.: InterVarsity Press, 2000.

Schneider, Floyd. *Evangelism for the Fainthearted*. Grand Rapids: Kregel Publications, 2000.

Shade, Patrick. *Habits of Hope: A Pragmatic Theory*. Nashville: Vanderbilt University Press, 2001.

Sire, James W.,. *The Universe Next Door: A Basic Worldview Catalog*. Kindle electronic edition ed. Downers Grove, Ill: InterVarsity Press, 1997.

Skreslet, Stanley H. *Picturing Christian Witness: New Testament Images of Disciples in Mission*. Grand Rapids: William B. Eerdmans Publishing Company, 2006.

Thompson Jr., W. Oscar. *Concentric Circles of Concern: Seven Stages for Making Disciples*. Nashville: Broadman & Holman Publishers, 1999.

Tinder, Glenn. *The Fabric of Hope: An Essay*. Atlanta: Scholars Press, 1999.

Turner, Matthew Paul. *The Coffeehouse Gospel: Sharing Your Faith in Everyday Conversation*. Lake Mary, FL: Relevant Books, 2004.

Wallace, David F. "David Foster Wallace on Life and Work." The Wall Street Journal. http://online.wsj.com/news/articles/SB122178211966454607 (accessed April 21, 2014).

Wojcicki, Edward. *A Crisis of Hope in the Modern World*. Chicago: The Thomas More Press, 1991.

Yankelovich, Daniel. *New Rules: Searching for Self-Fulfillment in a World Turned Upside Down*. New York: Random House, 1981.

ABOUT THE AUTHOR

Lee Rogers is passionate about connecting people to Jesus and equipping Christians to share their faith. He's served in full time youth ministry for 15 years in Philadelphia and Central Pennsylvania, and now works to catalyze a movement of students reaching students at school across Pennsylvania and Delaware. A gifted communicator and credentialed Life Coach, Lee speaks to thousands of people each year through school assemblies, retreats, and church services. He is a graduate of Valley Forge Christian College and holds a Master of Divinity from Regent University. He and his wife Christine love to travel, meet new people, and have great conversations.

CONTACT

Twitter: @TheLeeRogers
Facebook: fb.com/TheLeeRogers
Instagram: @TheLeeRogers